Mometrix

TEST PREPARATION

Virginia

SOL World History and Geography: 1500 A.D. to the Present

Secrets Study Guide

I0880196

Dear Future Exam Success Story

First of all, **THANK YOU** for purchasing Mometrix study materials!

Second, congratulations! You are one of the few determined test-takers who are committed to doing whatever it takes to excel on your exam. **You have come to the right place.** We developed these study materials with one goal in mind: to deliver you the information you need in a format that's concise and easy to use.

In addition to optimizing your guide for the content of the test, we've outlined our recommended steps for breaking down the preparation process into small, attainable goals so you can make sure you stay on track.

We've also analyzed the entire test-taking process, identifying the most common pitfalls and showing how you can overcome them and be ready for any curveball the test throws you.

Standardized testing is one of the biggest obstacles on your road to success, which only increases the importance of doing well in the high-pressure, high-stakes environment of test day. Your results on this test could have a significant impact on your future, and this guide provides the information and practical advice to help you achieve your full potential on test day.

Your success is our success

We would love to hear from you! If you would like to share the story of your exam success or if you have any questions or comments in regard to our products, please contact us at **800-673-8175** or **support@mometrix.com**.

Thanks again for your business and we wish you continued success!

Sincerely,
The Mometrix Test Preparation Team

Need more help? Check out our flashcards at:
http://MometrixFlashcards.com/SOL

Written and edited by the Mometrix Exam Secrets Test Prep Team
Printed in the United States of America

TABLE OF CONTENTS

Introduction

Thank you for purchasing this resource! You have made the choice to prepare yourself for a test that could have a huge impact on your future, and this guide is designed to help you be fully ready for test day. Obviously, it's important to have a solid understanding of the test material, but you also need to be prepared for the unique environment and stressors of the test, so that you can perform to the best of your abilities.

For this purpose, the first section that appears in this guide is the **Secret Keys**. We've devoted countless hours to meticulously researching what works and what doesn't, and we've boiled down our findings to the five most impactful steps you can take to improve your performance on the test. We start at the beginning with study planning and move through the preparation process, all the way to the testing strategies that will help you get the most out of what you know when you're finally sitting in front of the test.

We recommend that you start preparing for your test as far in advance as possible. However, if you've bought this guide as a last-minute study resource and only have a few days before your test, we recommend that you skip over the first two Secret Keys since they address a long-term study plan.

If you struggle with **test anxiety**, we strongly encourage you to check out our recommendations for how you can overcome it. Test anxiety is a formidable foe, but it can be beaten, and we want to make sure you have the tools you need to defeat it.

Secret Key #1 – Plan Big, Study Small

There's a lot riding on your performance. If you want to ace this test, you're going to need to keep your skills sharp and the material fresh in your mind. You need a plan that lets you review everything you need to know while still fitting in your schedule. We'll break this strategy down into three categories.

Information Organization

Start with the information you already have: the official test outline. From this, you can make a complete list of all the concepts you need to cover before the test. Organize these concepts into groups that can be studied together, and create a list of any related vocabulary you need to learn so you can brush up on any difficult terms. You'll want to keep this vocabulary list handy once you actually start studying since you may need to add to it along the way.

Time Management

Once you have your set of study concepts, decide how to spread them out over the time you have left before the test. Break your study plan into small, clear goals so you have a manageable task for each day and know exactly what you're doing. Then just focus on one small step at a time. When you manage your time this way, you don't need to spend hours at a time studying. Studying a small block of content for a short period each day helps you retain information better and avoid stressing over how much you have left to do. You can relax knowing that you have a plan to cover everything in time. In order for this strategy to be effective though, you have to start studying early and stick to your schedule. Avoid the exhaustion and futility that comes from last-minute cramming!

Study Environment

The environment you study in has a big impact on your learning. Studying in a coffee shop, while probably more enjoyable, is not likely to be as fruitful as studying in a quiet room. It's important to keep distractions to a minimum. You're only planning to study for a short block of time, so make the most of it. Don't pause to check your phone or get up to find a snack. It's also important to **avoid multitasking**. Research has consistently shown that multitasking will make your studying dramatically less effective. Your study area should also be comfortable and well-lit so you don't have the distraction of straining your eyes or sitting on an uncomfortable chair.

The time of day you study is also important. You want to be rested and alert. Don't wait until just before bedtime. Study when you'll be most likely to comprehend and remember. Even better, if you know what time of day your test will be, set that time aside for study. That way your brain will be used to working on that subject at that specific time and you'll have a better chance of recalling information.

Finally, it can be helpful to team up with others who are studying for the same test. Your actual studying should be done in as isolated an environment as possible, but the work of organizing the information and setting up the study plan can be divided up. In between study sessions, you can discuss with your teammates the concepts that you're all studying and quiz each other on the details. Just be sure that your teammates are as serious about the test as you are. If you find that your study time is being replaced with social time, you might need to find a new team.

Secret Key #2 – Make Your Studying Count

You're devoting a lot of time and effort to preparing for this test, so you want to be absolutely certain it will pay off. This means doing more than just reading the content and hoping you can remember it on test day. It's important to make every minute of study count. There are two main areas you can focus on to make your studying count.

Retention

It doesn't matter how much time you study if you can't remember the material. You need to make sure you are retaining the concepts. To check your retention of the information you're learning, try recalling it at later times with minimal prompting. Try carrying around flashcards and glance at one or two from time to time or ask a friend who's also studying for the test to quiz you.

To enhance your retention, look for ways to put the information into practice so that you can apply it rather than simply recalling it. If you're using the information in practical ways, it will be much easier to remember. Similarly, it helps to solidify a concept in your mind if you're not only reading it to yourself but also explaining it to someone else. Ask a friend to let you teach them about a concept you're a little shaky on (or speak aloud to an imaginary audience if necessary). As you try to summarize, define, give examples, and answer your friend's questions, you'll understand the concepts better and they will stay with you longer. Finally, step back for a big picture view and ask yourself how each piece of information fits with the whole subject. When you link the different concepts together and see them working together as a whole, it's easier to remember the individual components.

Finally, practice showing your work on any multi-step problems, even if you're just studying. Writing out each step you take to solve a problem will help solidify the process in your mind, and you'll be more likely to remember it during the test.

Modality

Modality simply refers to the means or method by which you study. Choosing a study modality that fits your own individual learning style is crucial. No two people learn best in exactly the same way, so it's important to know your strengths and use them to your advantage.

For example, if you learn best by visualization, focus on visualizing a concept in your mind and draw an image or a diagram. Try color-coding your notes, illustrating them, or creating symbols that will trigger your mind to recall a learned concept. If you learn best by hearing or discussing information, find a study partner who learns the same way or read aloud to yourself. Think about how to put the information in your own words. Imagine that you are giving a lecture on the topic and record yourself so you can listen to it later.

For any learning style, flashcards can be helpful. Organize the information so you can take advantage of spare moments to review. Underline key words or phrases. Use different colors for different categories. Mnemonic devices (such as creating a short list in which every item starts with the same letter) can also help with retention. Find what works best for you and use it to store the information in your mind most effectively and easily.

Secret Key #3 – Practice the Right Way

Your success on test day depends not only on how many hours you put into preparing, but also on whether you prepared the right way. It's good to check along the way to see if your studying is paying off. One of the most effective ways to do this is by taking practice tests to evaluate your progress. Practice tests are useful because they show exactly where you need to improve. Every time you take a practice test, pay special attention to these three groups of questions:

- The questions you got wrong
- The questions you had to guess on, even if you guessed right
- The questions you found difficult or slow to work through

This will show you exactly what your weak areas are, and where you need to devote more study time. Ask yourself why each of these questions gave you trouble. Was it because you didn't understand the material? Was it because you didn't remember the vocabulary? Do you need more repetitions on this type of question to build speed and confidence? Dig into those questions and figure out how you can strengthen your weak areas as you go back to review the material.

Additionally, many practice tests have a section explaining the answer choices. It can be tempting to read the explanation and think that you now have a good understanding of the concept. However, an explanation likely only covers part of the question's broader context. Even if the explanation makes perfect sense, **go back and investigate** every concept related to the question until you're positive you have a thorough understanding.

As you go along, keep in mind that the practice test is just that: practice. Memorizing these questions and answers will not be very helpful on the actual test because it is unlikely to have any of the same exact questions. If you only know the right answers to the sample questions, you won't be prepared for the real thing. **Study the concepts** until you understand them fully, and then you'll be able to answer any question that shows up on the test.

It's important to wait on the practice tests until you're ready. If you take a test on your first day of study, you may be overwhelmed by the amount of material covered and how much you need to learn. Work up to it gradually.

On test day, you'll need to be prepared for answering questions, managing your time, and using the test-taking strategies you've learned. It's a lot to balance, like a mental marathon that will have a big impact on your future. Like training for a marathon, you'll need to start slowly and work your way up. When test day arrives, you'll be ready.

Start with the strategies you've read in the first two Secret Keys—plan your course and study in the way that works best for you. If you have time, consider using multiple study resources to get different approaches to the same concepts. It can be helpful to see difficult concepts from more than one angle. Then find a good source for practice tests. Many times, the test website will suggest potential study resources or provide sample tests.

Practice Test Strategy

If you're able to find at least three practice tests, we recommend this strategy:

Untimed and Open-Book Practice

Take the first test with no time constraints and with your notes and study guide handy. Take your time and focus on applying the strategies you've learned.

Timed and Open-Book Practice

Take the second practice test open-book as well, but set a timer and practice pacing yourself to finish in time.

Timed and Closed-Book Practice

Take any other practice tests as if it were test day. Set a timer and put away your study materials. Sit at a table or desk in a quiet room, imagine yourself at the testing center, and answer questions as quickly and accurately as possible.

Keep repeating timed and closed-book tests on a regular basis until you run out of practice tests or it's time for the actual test. Your mind will be ready for the schedule and stress of test day, and you'll be able to focus on recalling the material you've learned.

Secret Key #4 – Pace Yourself

Once you're fully prepared for the material on the test, your biggest challenge on test day will be managing your time. Just knowing that the clock is ticking can make you panic even if you have plenty of time left. Work on pacing yourself so you can build confidence against the time constraints of the exam. Pacing is a difficult skill to master, especially in a high-pressure environment, so **practice is vital**.

Set time expectations for your pace based on how much time is available. For example, if a section has 60 questions and the time limit is 30 minutes, you know you have to average 30 seconds or less per question in order to answer them all. Although 30 seconds is the hard limit, set 25 seconds per question as your goal, so you reserve extra time to spend on harder questions. When you budget extra time for the harder questions, you no longer have any reason to stress when those questions take longer to answer.

Don't let this time expectation distract you from working through the test at a calm, steady pace, but keep it in mind so you don't spend too much time on any one question. Recognize that taking extra time on one question you don't understand may keep you from answering two that you do understand later in the test. If your time limit for a question is up and you're still not sure of the answer, mark it and move on, and come back to it later if the time and the test format allow. If the testing format doesn't allow you to return to earlier questions, just make an educated guess; then put it out of your mind and move on.

On the easier questions, be careful not to rush. It may seem wise to hurry through them so you have more time for the challenging ones, but it's not worth missing one if you know the concept and just didn't take the time to read the question fully. Work efficiently but make sure you understand the question and have looked at all of the answer choices, since more than one may seem right at first.

Even if you're paying attention to the time, you may find yourself a little behind at some point. You should speed up to get back on track, but do so wisely. Don't panic; just take a few seconds less on each question until you're caught up. Don't guess without thinking, but do look through the answer choices and eliminate any you know are wrong. If you can get down to two choices, it is often worthwhile to guess from those. Once you've chosen an answer, move on and don't dwell on any that you skipped or had to hurry through. If a question was taking too long, chances are it was one of the harder ones, so you weren't as likely to get it right anyway.

On the other hand, if you find yourself getting ahead of schedule, it may be beneficial to slow down a little. The more quickly you work, the more likely you are to make a careless mistake that will affect your score. You've budgeted time for each question, so don't be afraid to spend that time. Practice an efficient but careful pace to get the most out of the time you have.

Secret Key #5 – Have a Plan for Guessing

When you're taking the test, you may find yourself stuck on a question. Some of the answer choices seem better than others, but you don't see the one answer choice that is obviously correct. What do you do?

The scenario described above is very common, yet most test takers have not effectively prepared for it. Developing and practicing a plan for guessing may be one of the single most effective uses of your time as you get ready for the exam.

In developing your plan for guessing, there are three questions to address:

- When should you start the guessing process?
- How should you narrow down the choices?
- Which answer should you choose?

When to Start the Guessing Process

Unless your plan for guessing is to select C every time (which, despite its merits, is not what we recommend), you need to leave yourself enough time to apply your answer elimination strategies. Since you have a limited amount of time for each question, that means that if you're going to give yourself the best shot at guessing correctly, you have to decide quickly whether or not you will guess.

Of course, the best-case scenario is that you don't have to guess at all, so first, see if you can answer the question based on your knowledge of the subject and basic reasoning skills. Focus on the key words in the question and try to jog your memory of related topics. Give yourself a chance to bring the knowledge to mind, but once you realize that you don't have (or you can't access) the knowledge you need to answer the question, it's time to start the guessing process.

It's almost always better to start the guessing process too early than too late. It only takes a few seconds to remember something and answer the question from knowledge. Carefully eliminating wrong answer choices takes longer. Plus, going through the process of eliminating answer choices can actually help jog your memory.

Summary: Start the guessing process as soon as you decide that you can't answer the question based on your knowledge.

How to Narrow Down the Choices

The next chapter in this book (**Test-Taking Strategies**) includes a wide range of strategies for how to approach questions and how to look for answer choices to eliminate. You will definitely want to read those carefully, practice them, and figure out which ones work best for you. Here though, we're going to address a mindset rather than a particular strategy.

Your odds of guessing an answer correctly depend on how many options you are choosing from.

Number of options left	5	4	3	2	1
Odds of guessing correctly	20%	25%	33%	50%	100%

You can see from this chart just how valuable it is to be able to eliminate incorrect answers and make an educated guess, but there are two things that many test takers do that cause them to miss out on the benefits of guessing:

- Accidentally eliminating the correct answer
- Selecting an answer based on an impression

We'll look at the first one here, and the second one in the next section.

To avoid accidentally eliminating the correct answer, we recommend a thought exercise called **the $5 challenge**. In this challenge, you only eliminate an answer choice from contention if you are willing to bet $5 on it being wrong. Why $5? Five dollars is a small but not insignificant amount of money. It's an amount you could afford to lose but wouldn't want to throw away. And while losing $5 once might not hurt too much, doing it twenty times will set you back $100. In the same way, each small decision you make—eliminating a choice here, guessing on a question there—won't by itself impact your score very much, but when you put them all together, they can make a big difference. By holding each answer choice elimination decision to a higher standard, you can reduce the risk of accidentally eliminating the correct answer.

The $5 challenge can also be applied in a positive sense: If you are willing to bet $5 that an answer choice *is* correct, go ahead and mark it as correct.

Summary: Only eliminate an answer choice if you are willing to bet $5 that it is wrong.

Which Answer to Choose

You're taking the test. You've run into a hard question and decided you'll have to guess. You've eliminated all the answer choices you're willing to bet $5 on. Now you have to pick an answer. Why do we even need to talk about this? Why can't you just pick whichever one you feel like when the time comes?

The answer to these questions is that if you don't come into the test with a plan, you'll rely on your impression to select an answer choice, and if you do that, you risk falling into a trap. The test writers know that everyone who takes their test will be guessing on some of the questions, so they intentionally write wrong answer choices to seem plausible. You still have to pick an answer though, and if the wrong answer choices are designed to look right, how can you ever be sure that you're not falling for their trap? The best solution we've found to this dilemma is to take the decision out of your hands entirely. Here is the process we recommend:

Once you've eliminated any choices that you are confident (willing to bet $5) are wrong, select the first remaining choice as your answer.

Whether you choose to select the first remaining choice, the second, or the last, the important thing is that you use some preselected standard. Using this approach guarantees that you will not be enticed into selecting an answer choice that looks right, because you are not basing your decision on how the answer choices look.

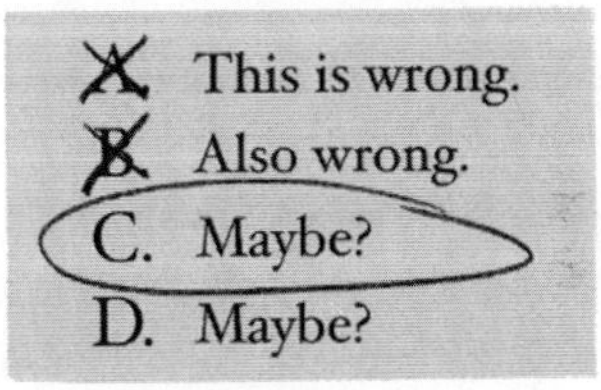

This is not meant to make you question your knowledge. Instead, it is to help you recognize the difference between your knowledge and your impressions. There's a huge difference between thinking an answer is right because of what you know, and thinking an answer is right because it looks or sounds like it should be right.

Summary: To ensure that your selection is appropriately random, make a predetermined selection from among all answer choices you have not eliminated.

Test-Taking Strategies

This section contains a list of test-taking strategies that you may find helpful as you work through the test. By taking what you know and applying logical thought, you can maximize your chances of answering any question correctly!

It is very important to realize that every question is different and every person is different: no single strategy will work on every question, and no single strategy will work for every person. That's why we've included all of them here, so you can try them out and determine which ones work best for different types of questions and which ones work best for you.

Question Strategies

☑ Read Carefully

Read the question and the answer choices carefully. Don't miss the question because you misread the terms. You have plenty of time to read each question thoroughly and make sure you understand what is being asked. Yet a happy medium must be attained, so don't waste too much time. You must read carefully and efficiently.

☑ Contextual Clues

Look for contextual clues. If the question includes a word you are not familiar with, look at the immediate context for some indication of what the word might mean. Contextual clues can often give you all the information you need to decipher the meaning of an unfamiliar word. Even if you can't determine the meaning, you may be able to narrow down the possibilities enough to make a solid guess at the answer to the question.

☑ Prefixes

If you're having trouble with a word in the question or answer choices, try dissecting it. Take advantage of every clue that the word might include. Prefixes can be a huge help. Usually, they allow you to determine a basic meaning. *Pre-* means before, *post-* means after, *pro-* is positive, *de-* is negative. From prefixes, you can get an idea of the general meaning of the word and try to put it into context.

☑ Hedge Words

Watch out for critical hedge words, such as *likely, may, can, often, almost, mostly, usually, generally, rarely,* and *sometimes.* Question writers insert these hedge phrases to cover every possibility. Often an answer choice will be wrong simply because it leaves no room for exception. Be on guard for answer choices that have definitive words such as *exactly* and *always.*

☑ Switchback Words

Stay alert for *switchbacks.* These are the words and phrases frequently used to alert you to shifts in thought. The most common switchback words are *but, although,* and *however.* Others include *nevertheless, on the other hand, even though, while, in spite of, despite,* and *regardless of.* Switchback words are important to catch because they can change the direction of the question or an answer choice.

⊘ FACE VALUE

When in doubt, use common sense. Accept the situation in the problem at face value. Don't read too much into it. These problems will not require you to make wild assumptions. If you have to go beyond creativity and warp time or space in order to have an answer choice fit the question, then you should move on and consider the other answer choices. These are normal problems rooted in reality. The applicable relationship or explanation may not be readily apparent, but it is there for you to figure out. Use your common sense to interpret anything that isn't clear.

Answer Choice Strategies

⊘ ANSWER SELECTION

The most thorough way to pick an answer choice is to identify and eliminate wrong answers until only one is left, then confirm it is the correct answer. Sometimes an answer choice may immediately seem right, but be careful. The test writers will usually put more than one reasonable answer choice on each question, so take a second to read all of them and make sure that the other choices are not equally obvious. As long as you have time left, it is better to read every answer choice than to pick the first one that looks right without checking the others.

⊘ ANSWER CHOICE FAMILIES

An answer choice family consists of two (in rare cases, three) answer choices that are very similar in construction and cannot all be true at the same time. If you see two answer choices that are direct opposites or parallels, one of them is usually the correct answer. For instance, if one answer choice says that quantity *x* increases and another either says that quantity *x* decreases (opposite) or says that quantity *y* increases (parallel), then those answer choices would fall into the same family. An answer choice that doesn't match the construction of the answer choice family is more likely to be incorrect. Most questions will not have answer choice families, but when they do appear, you should be prepared to recognize them.

⊘ ELIMINATE ANSWERS

Eliminate answer choices as soon as you realize they are wrong, but make sure you consider all possibilities. If you are eliminating answer choices and realize that the last one you are left with is also wrong, don't panic. Start over and consider each choice again. There may be something you missed the first time that you will realize on the second pass.

⊘ AVOID FACT TRAPS

Don't be distracted by an answer choice that is factually true but doesn't answer the question. You are looking for the choice that answers the question. Stay focused on what the question is asking for so you don't accidentally pick an answer that is true but incorrect. Always go back to the question and make sure the answer choice you've selected actually answers the question and is not merely a true statement.

⊘ EXTREME STATEMENTS

In general, you should avoid answers that put forth extreme actions as standard practice or proclaim controversial ideas as established fact. An answer choice that states the "process should be used in certain situations, if…" is much more likely to be correct than one that states the "process should be discontinued completely." The first is a calm rational statement and doesn't even make a definitive, uncompromising stance, using a hedge word *if* to provide wiggle room, whereas the second choice is far more extreme.

☑ Benchmark

As you read through the answer choices and you come across one that seems to answer the question well, mentally select that answer choice. This is not your final answer, but it's the one that will help you evaluate the other answer choices. The one that you selected is your benchmark or standard for judging each of the other answer choices. Every other answer choice must be compared to your benchmark. That choice is correct until proven otherwise by another answer choice beating it. If you find a better answer, then that one becomes your new benchmark. Once you've decided that no other choice answers the question as well as your benchmark, you have your final answer.

☑ Predict the Answer

Before you even start looking at the answer choices, it is often best to try to predict the answer. When you come up with the answer on your own, it is easier to avoid distractions and traps because you will know exactly what to look for. The right answer choice is unlikely to be word-for-word what you came up with, but it should be a close match. Even if you are confident that you have the right answer, you should still take the time to read each option before moving on.

General Strategies

☑ Tough Questions

If you are stumped on a problem or it appears too hard or too difficult, don't waste time. Move on! Remember though, if you can quickly check for obviously incorrect answer choices, your chances of guessing correctly are greatly improved. Before you completely give up, at least try to knock out a couple of possible answers. Eliminate what you can and then guess at the remaining answer choices before moving on.

☑ Check Your Work

Since you will probably not know every term listed and the answer to every question, it is important that you get credit for the ones that you do know. Don't miss any questions through careless mistakes. If at all possible, try to take a second to look back over your answer selection and make sure you've selected the correct answer choice and haven't made a costly careless mistake (such as marking an answer choice that you didn't mean to mark). This quick double check should more than pay for itself in caught mistakes for the time it costs.

☑ Pace Yourself

It's easy to be overwhelmed when you're looking at a page full of questions; your mind is confused and full of random thoughts, and the clock is ticking down faster than you would like. Calm down and maintain the pace that you have set for yourself. Especially as you get down to the last few minutes of the test, don't let the small numbers on the clock make you panic. As long as you are on track by monitoring your pace, you are guaranteed to have time for each question.

☑ Don't Rush

It is very easy to make errors when you are in a hurry. Maintaining a fast pace in answering questions is pointless if it makes you miss questions that you would have gotten right otherwise. Test writers like to include distracting information and wrong answers that seem right. Taking a little extra time to avoid careless mistakes can make all the difference in your test score. Find a pace that allows you to be confident in the answers that you select.

⊘ Keep Moving

Panicking will not help you pass the test, so do your best to stay calm and keep moving. Taking deep breaths and going through the answer elimination steps you practiced can help to break through a stress barrier and keep your pace.

Final Notes

The combination of a solid foundation of content knowledge and the confidence that comes from practicing your plan for applying that knowledge is the key to maximizing your performance on test day. As your foundation of content knowledge is built up and strengthened, you'll find that the strategies included in this chapter become more and more effective in helping you quickly sift through the distractions and traps of the test to isolate the correct answer.

Now that you're preparing to move forward into the test content chapters of this book, be sure to keep your goal in mind. As you read, think about how you will be able to apply this information on the test. If you've already seen sample questions for the test and you have an idea of the question format and style, try to come up with questions of your own that you can answer based on what you're reading. This will give you valuable practice applying your knowledge in the same ways you can expect to on test day.

Good luck and good studying!

Age of Revolutions

Scientific Revolution

The rapid advance in learning known as the Scientific Revolution was a product of the systematic form of inquiry known as the scientific method. With the scientific method, learning is incremental: a question is posed, a hypothetical solution is offered, observations are made, and the hypothesis is either supported or refuted. The consistency of the method made it easy for scientific discoveries to be transferred from one country to another. Along with a standardized form of measurement, the development of the scientific method gave scientists a common language. Scientists also benefited from the development of powerful telescopes and microscopes.

Major Figures of the Scientific Revolution

After Copernicus startled the world by challenging the geocentric (that is, earth-centered) model for the universe, the Italian Galileo Galilei supplied scientific experiments that proved the accuracy of Copernicus' theory. One of the philosophical heroes of the Scientific Revolution was the Frenchman Rene Descartes, who attempted to base his beliefs about the world upon empirical and provable facts: most famously, "I think, therefore I am." Francis Bacon was an English intellectual who wrote copiously on the possibilities for science to improve the human condition. Sir Isaac Newton excelled in many fields, but is best known for his theories of motion and gravitation. Newton helped create the general idea that objects in the world behave in regular and predictable ways.

Enlightenment

Between the years 1600 and 1770, political and social philosophy in Europe underwent a tremendous change, known collectively as the Enlightenment. Just as Northern Italy had been the center of the Renaissance, so now Paris was the hub of progressive thought. The collection of philosophes, who sought to bring every subject under the authority of reason, included both deists (those who believed in God) and atheists (those who did not). The study known as political science first emerged during this period. Intellectuals began to question the divine right that had been claimed by absolute monarchs in the past; they sought to determine which was the best form of government for all the citizens of the country.

Peace of Westphalia and Louis XIV

The monarchs of the Enlightenment period found themselves under increasing pressure to be tolerant and benevolent. In Western Europe, so-called "enlightened despots" governed in order to promote the best interests of their subjects; this was probably done more to retain power than to express any profound solidarity with the commoners. France had become the central power on the European continent after the Peace of Westphalia (1648), which ended the Thirty Years' War and weakened Germany. The long reign of Louis XIV of France was characterized by grandiosity and the cultivation of the arts. Louis spent considerable effort trying to acquire new territories for France and glory for himself, and so alarmed the other European powers with his swiftness from victory to victory that many former enemies allied against France.

Major Figures of the Enlightenment

One of the most sparkling wits of the Enlightenment period belonged to the Frenchman Voltaire (1694-1778). He challenged the authority of the Church, declaring that people should tolerate the views of others and that no one man or group had a monopoly on absolute truth. Thomas Hobbes (1598-1679) was one of the most influential political theorists of the period. In his masterpiece

"Leviathan," he declared that the base impulses of the people had to be restrained by a powerful and just monarch. John Locke (1632-1704), on the other hand, declared that men were born with natural rights which could not be justly denied them. Rousseau (1712-78), a Swiss philosopher, asserted that the government only ruled so long as it did so to the satisfaction of the General Will of the people.

Rule of Peter the Great and Catherine the Great

Peter the Great (1672-1725) was responsible for the transformation of Russia from an impoverished agricultural nation to a strong commercial nation. Peter was enamored of the ways of the western European nations, and made several trips to other capitals to learn the intricacies of Enlightenment politics and trade. St. Petersburg was intended to be a Russian city in the style of Paris or Berlin. Peter's innovations revitalized the economy, but they also set a standard for decadence that would be carried on by future czars. Catherine II, otherwise known as Catherine the Great, ruled from 1762 to 1796 and implemented many Enlightenment policies in education and the arts. Nevertheless, in the remote provinces of Russia the feudal system endured, and the economy remained stunted.

Prussia

The Peace of Westphalia (1648) established the independence of several small sections of Germany; chief among these new states was Prussia. Frederick the Great (1712-86) became the ruler of Prussia in 1740 and displayed marvelous efficiency and benevolence. He made a genuine effort to allow for the coexistence of all the religious groups in Prussia, and also worked to improve the lives of the serfs. Frederick also encouraged immigration to Prussia, which brought in new ideas and technological advances. Prussia, which had long suffered economically because of its lack of a coastline, now became a producer of luxury goods like porcelain and silk.

Taiping Rebellion

The Taiping Rebellion lasted in China between the years 1850 and 1864. It was a religious and political rebellion against the government of the Manchus, led by the Christian Hung Hsiu-chuan. The rebels advocated the public ownership of land and a self-sufficient economy. They wanted to rid China of the encroaching influences of foreign merchants. Hung's troops were able to conquer Nanking and make it the capital of their "Great Peaceful Heavenly Dynasty." Internal feuds weakened the Taiping, however, and the western powers (concerned that they would lose the Chinese market) helped to oust them in 1864. The Taiping Rebellion was by far the bloodiest war of the nineteenth century.

Opium War

The Opium War lasted between the years 1839 and 1842. It began because the British kept trafficking opium from India into China because they wanted to trade with the Chinese, and opium was the only product that China could not produce for itself. The Chinese government, however, was appalled by the effect that the drug had on its citizens, and mounted a serious anti-opium campaign. When British merchants appealed to their leaders, the British navy was sent in order to force the Chinese to accept the opium. The British ended up seizing several Chinese cities, including Shanghai and Nanking. The war ended with the Treaty of Nanking in 1842; China was forced to cede Hong Kong to the British, and several Chinese ports had to be left open for trade.

Meiji Reform

In 1854, an American group led by Commodore Matthew Perry forced Japan to open its ports to foreign merchants. Japan had been closed to the West for 200 years. The Japanese people were not pleased with this development, and they blamed the Tokugawa shogun (the military leader of the period). In 1867, the shogun resigned and Emperor Matsuhito declared that he was now in charge. The Japanese capital was moved from Kyoto to Edo (which was renamed Tokyo). The ensuing period in Japanese history is known as the Meiji Period. During it, the feudal system was abolished, and Western ideas became popular. The samurai had their land right revoked and were eventually eliminated altogether. In the late nineteenth century, Japanese leaders began to turn their attentions to expansion onto the Asian continent; in the Sino-Japanese war, they conquered parts of China and Korea.

Boxer Rebellion

The Boxer Rebellion was a peasant uprising in China around the turn of the twentieth century. The aims of the rebels were to overthrow the Manchu government and to cast all foreigners out of China. The rebels were known as the Boxers because they practiced certain mystical boxing rituals. After Japan had defeated China in 1895, the Japanese had exercised a great deal of influence on the Chinese economy. Around 1900, Boxers began to kill foreign merchants and diplomats. An international force was assembled to defeat the Boxers. During the ensuing fight the city of Peking was almost entirely destroyed. Eventually, the western powers prevailed and forced the Boxer leaders to sign an incredibly unfavorable treaty.

French Revolution

Aware of the injustice of the French tax policy, King Louis XVI tried to pass some reforms but was repeatedly thwarted by the greedy nobles and clergy. The Third Estate was infuriated, and refused to vote in the Estates General anymore. Instead, prominent members of the middle class banded together to form the National Assembly, which purported to represent the interests of common Frenchmen. At the same time, the peasants were in full revolt. On July 14, 1789, they stormed the Parisian prison known as the Bastille. The success of this riot inspired more peasants to clamor for representation, and the diversion it caused kept the government from dealing with the National Assembly.

Causes of the French Revolution

Before the revolution, France was governed by an absolute monarch and with regard to matters of taxation, the Estates General, which had been formed in order to represent the common people. The Estates general was composed of three estates: the clergy (First Estate), nobility (Second Estate), and everyone else (Third Estate). Unfortunately, this body had been marginalized by a series of powerful monarchs, and it was arranged such that the largest group by far, the Third Estate, only had one-third of the vote. In any case, the Third Estate usually found its desires opposed by the other estates. Another source of anger for the middle class and peasants was the tax structure; the nobles and clergy were not forced to pay taxes, and thus the burden of France's depressed economy fell upon the Third Estate.

Reign of Terror

As the government established by the Third Estate descended into chaos, the radical Jacobin leader Robespierre took charge. He had an idealistic vision of what France could become, and he was willing to kill thousands in order to see it realized. The guillotine provided a swift way to execute scores of opponents, a group that included anyone who dared challenge the Jacobin party line or was suspected of retaining their Catholic faith in the new culture of state-mandated atheism. Among those executed were King Louis XVI and his wife, Marie Antoinette. After a while, the French tired of the violence and turmoil of the Reign of Terror, and Robespierre himself fell victim to the guillotine. A group of five prominent men, known as the Directory, was established to restore calm. This group would last until 1799, when it was overthrown in a coup that would eventually bring Napoleon Bonaparte to power.

Declaration of the Rights of Man

After the storming of the Bastille and the formation of the National Assembly in 1789, the French middle and lower classes joined together and established a new government with the slogan "Liberty, Equality, Fraternity." This government quickly reformed the tax code and declared that government offices would henceforth be filled on the basis of merit. The National Assembly also eliminated serfdom and drafted a Declaration of the Rights of Man, which was similar to the American Bill of Rights. The National Assembly then seized the lands that belonged to the Church, and eliminated the feudal rights of the aristocracy. Soon, there was dissension within the Third Estate, and the revolution became more radical and violent.

Napoleon Bonaparte

Napoleon Bonaparte (1769-1821) began his career as a French military commander, scoring major victories in Austria and England. Upon his return to the chaos of France, he led a coup and was installed as the leader of France. He was subsequently elected by a popular vote. Almost immediately, Napoleon reformed French education, agriculture, and infrastructure. The main object of Napoleon's rule, however, was the acquisition of territory both in Europe and in the New World. Napoleon's troops quickly conquered Austria, Portugal, Spain, and Prussia. Napoleon, who modeled himself after Charlemagne in many ways, then crowned himself emperor. The French empire proved too large to manage, however, and Napoleon further weakened himself with a disastrous campaign against Russia.

Fall of Napoleon

After Napoleon's debacle in Russia debilitated his military, revolts sprung up in many of the nations that he had conquered, and Napoleon was overthrown. The leaders of the countries that had overthrown Napoleon met in Vienna to decide how to respond to him. These three men, Prince von Metternich of Austria, the English Duke of Wellington, and Alexander I of Russia, were constantly in disagreement, however, and Napoleon used this opportunity to return from his exile on the Isle of Elba in the Mediterranean and reclaim power. Finally, Napoleon was defeated at Waterloo and sent into permanent exile. The allies met again at the Congress of Vienna in 1815 where France was not treated too harshly, and it was determined that a balance of power should be maintained in Europe to ensure that no one in the future tried to dominate the Continent.

Industrial Revolution

The Industrial Revolution in Europe in the nineteenth century produced immediate and far-reaching changes in the social structure. England was perhaps the first to feel the effects of rapid industrialization; the factory system for manufacturing textiles was implemented, meaning that individuals were only required to do one in the series of tasks required to prepare a piece of cloth. This division of labor increased productivity. New energy sources, such as the steam engine, also made fabulous increases in productivity possible. Coal was introduced as an aid to the iron-smelting process, and the mass production of cotton textiles was soon propelling the English economy.

Working class and Luddites

As people flooded the cities to work in the booming factories, large landowners consolidated the farmlands they left behind. Working class individuals were probably not pleased with their new lives: 18-hour days, low wages, and dangerous machinery were among the problems faced by this new underclass. Oftentimes, women and children were employed for the most menial jobs, and they were paid less than men. A small rebellion, led by a group called the Luddites, tried to resist the tide of industrialization and were known for vandalizing factory equipment. Still, most individuals were enticed by the prospect of upward mobility that the new, fluid class system offered, and were willing to endure hardship in exchange for hope.

Social changes during the Industrial Revolution

With the success of the textile industry, more and more workers were needed in the European cities, and therefore people began to abandon their country lives and take factory jobs in town. This rapid urbanization created a new middle class in Europe, and it also created a number of problems. Most cities did not have the infrastructure to support such an explosion in population, and as such disease, crime, and poverty were common. The booming success of industry made many people rich as investors and merchants, and therefore the middle class assumed even more political power in Europe. Social mobility was infinitely more possible in this economic environment, encouraging many people to stick with jobs that were demeaning and not especially lucrative.

Independence struggle in Latin America

When Spain fell to Napoleon's forces in 1809, the provinces of Chile and Buenos Aires both declared themselves independent. At this time, Peru was the stronghold of Spanish power in the New World, and therefore the rebels attacked the government there. Led by the Argentinean Jose San Martin, rebels entered Lima and declared Peru an independent state in 1821. The greatest military leader of the independence movement, however, was Simon Bolivar. He had traveled extensively in Europe, and used his knowledge of the enemy to run the Spaniards out of Colombia, Venezuela, and Central America. Bolivar eventually seized control of Peru, and hoped to form a great union of South American nations, but this alliance was eventually torn asunder by internal feuds.

19th century Europe

Emergence of classical liberalism

The political and economic philosophies of the Enlightenment gave rise in the nineteenth century to classical liberalism. Adam Smith summarized the classical liberal view of economics in his book "The Wealth of Nations"; there Smith invoked the idea of the "invisible hand" to suggest that markets, if left alone, would regulate themselves. Smith endorsed the changes brought on by the Industrial Revolution as part of the natural evolution of the capitalist economy. Thomas Malthus is another intellectual whose ideas contributed to classical liberalism; he declared that the world was in danger of becoming overpopulated, and that the natural solution would be for the poor to die of disease and starvation. Malthus, too, tacitly supported the Industrial Revolution by suggesting that the plight of the poor was in the best interest of humanity.

Emergence of nationalism

In the nineteenth century, the spirit of nationalism that had been building in Europe since the Middle Ages reached a critical mass. Nationalism refers to pride in the traditions, culture, language, and past of a certain nation of people, and not necessarily to pride in one's country. This is important to note, because in the 19th century there were many nations of people thrown together as parts of a larger kingdom. The rising tide of nationalism, then, was a concern to the ruling monarchs, who hoped to hold together disparate nations under their control. Russia, for instance, contained a wide variety of cultures and languages under one leadership.

Emergence of socialism

Socialism is a political philosophy which declares that the economic means of production should be owned by the workers. This control may either be exercised directly by the workers through local councils, or by the state with the consent of the workers. Socialists hope thereby to create a state of social equality and an even distribution of wealth. Not surprisingly, this movement was most popular among the working classes in nineteenth-century Europe. Socialists at this time declared that capitalism served only the interests of the very wealthy, and exploited everyone else. In their view, a socialist society would provide a greater reward for hard work, and would create harmonious societies.

Emergence of Social Liberalism

Social liberalism developed in the late nineteenth century as an alternative to classical liberalism. Social liberalism declares that political problems can be solved by the work of liberal institutions in the government. Unlike the classical liberals, social liberals believe that the government should exercise some influence on the economy, and should extend some basic welfare services to the people. The aim of social liberalism was to improve life for the poor and disadvantaged. Social liberals were also very outspoken on issues of civil rights and individual liberties. Some of the most famous social liberals are Jeremy Bentham, John Stuart Mill, and John Dewey.

Emergence of Marxism

The political theories of socialism and communism both take their inspiration from the works of Karl Marx (1818-83). Marx declared that economics have been the primary determinant in history, and that the history of society is nothing more than a "history of class struggle." Marx asserts that problems have been created in situations where the material that a worker produces is worth more than the compensation he receives for his work. The surplus goes to the capitalist owner, and the worker is caught in a situation where he can never get ahead. The inevitable result, according to Marx, is a revolution of the working class (which he called the proletariat), and the installation of an economic system similar to socialism or communism.

19th Century British Politics

During the nineteenth century, the memory of Napoleon and the balance of power established by the Congress of Vienna prevented any large conflicts. The Industrial Revolution had made Britain the wealthiest and most powerful nation in Europe. The rise of a rich middle class caused the British Parliament to alter voting laws so that more of the wealthy would have influence. This was done with the Reform Act of 1832; in 1833, Britain abolished slavery in its colonies. This was not enough for the many working-class Britons, however, and they lobbied long and hard for universal suffrage, until it was finally granted in the 1880's. The British movement for universal suffrage was known as Chartism.

19th Century German Politics

Ever since the end of Charlemagne's empire, Austria and Germany had not been unified as a single nation. This was finally achieved by the Prussian Otto von Bismarck after a long period of suppression of German nationalists. Bismarck's unification of Prussia was mainly aimed at defeating the rival Hapsburgs, who controlled Austria. When Prussia won the Austro-Prussian and Franco-Prussian wars in quick succession, Bismarck declared that he had achieved his ends and unified the German empire. He oversaw the creation of the Reichstag, a legislative body that would provide representation to the middle and lower classes. Germany threw itself into the project of industrialization.

19th Century French Politics

Internal turmoil caused France to miss out on much of the wealth of the Industrial Revolution. After the demise of Napoleon, Louis XVII had been restored to the throne by the Congress of Vienna. He was succeeded by the arch-conservative Charles X, who was quite unpopular and was chased off the throne in the July Revolution of 1830. In his place came Louis Philippe, who administered over a fairly stable country for eighteen years until he was deposed in the revolution of 1848. Next came

Napoleon III: elected the emperor of France in 1851, he remained in power until the French defeat in the Franco-Prussian War of 1870. From 1870 until 1940, France would be governed by a constitutional and democratic government which was for the most part conservative.

19TH CENTURY RUSSIAN POLITICS

At the beginning of the nineteenth century, much of Russia was still mired in an impoverished, quasi-feudal state. After the death of Alexander in 1825, the Decembrists tried to force the incoming Czar to adopt a constitution allocating some power to the people. This next Czar was Nicholas I, who used a secret police to try to eliminate the roots of the popular insurrection. This policy of suppression only further isolated Russia from the rest of Europe, which was at that time reducing the power of the monarch. Russia later lost the Crimean War to Britain, France, and the Ottoman Empire, and many Russians bemoaned the backward state of their country. Finally, a new czar, Alexander II, freed the serfs and tried to industrialize. This happened slowly.

19TH CENTURY ITALIAN POLITICS

Italy, like Germany, had really been more of a disjointed collection of independent city-states than a nation in its own right. In the nineteenth century, however, there was a drive to unify the region. A leader from the Piedmont region, Camillo Cavour, tried to bring the various city-states together through diplomacy rather than combat. This process took a very long time, but was eventually completed in the 1870s. Northern Italy, which had intimate contact with Germany, became industrialized during this period, and the city of Milan enjoyed immense growth. Southern Italy, on the other hand, remained largely rural. This distinction between the two halves of Italy would be a source of conflict in the future.

RUSSIAN REVOLUTION OF 1905

At the turn of the twentieth century, Russia was torn by the trends of industrialism and imperialism. Russia, despite still being an absolute monarchy, was trying to modernize its cities. In other words, Russia was attempting to create all of the economic changes of Western Europe without allowing any of the accompanying social changes. Russians were also disheartened by the defeat of their navy in the Russo-Japanese War. The socialist party in Russia, known as the Bolsheviks, began to lead revolts against the Mensheviks. When a peaceful demonstration against the Czar was brutally suppressed, the rebels became energized. The Russian Revolution of 1905, as this was known, continued with revolts by peasants and soldiers, until the czar promised to create a constitutional monarchy with a powerful legislative body, known as the Duma.

Emergence of a Global Age

Renaissance

Beginning of the Renaissance

In the 14th century, the turmoil caused by war and plague weakened the power of Christian theology. In its place came the philosophy of humanism, in which the emphasis is placed on individual potential and determination while detracting from one's attention to the realm of the divine. Humanist thought contributed to a resurgence in the arts and sciences, which eventually came to be known as the Renaissance. In the 14th and 15th centuries, the center of this resurgence was in Northern Italy, in large part because this was the crossroads of several important trade routes. Specifically, the city-states of Milan, Florence, and Venice cultivated excellent artists. Talented youths typically studied in these cities with their expenses paid by a wealthy patron; the most famous patrons were the Medici family in Florence.

Italian Artists of the Renaissance

The early part of the Renaissance was dominated by the artists congregated in Northern Italy. Among them were several immortal talents. Donatello (1386-1466) sculpted a marvelous David, and was the first artist in this period to depict the naked human body (religious concerns had kept recent artists from doing so). Botticelli (1444-1510) is the painter of the famous Birth of Venus. Leonardo da Vinci (1452-1519) excelled in a number of different fields, but he is perhaps best known for painting the Mona Lisa and the Last Supper. Michelangelo (1475-1563), though, was probably the most famous painter and sculptor of the time; he painted the ceiling in the Sistine Chapel and sculpted the most famous David.

Age of Exploration

At the same time that the Renaissance was reinvigorating European cultural life, a desire to explore the world abroad was growing. Indeed, the ability to make long voyages was facilitated by the advances in navigational technology made around this time. The main reason for exploration, though, was economic. Europeans had first been introduced to eastern goods during the Crusades, and the exploits of Marco Polo in the 13th century had further whetted the western appetite for contact with distant lands. This increasing focus on exploration and trade caused a general shift in the balance of power in Europe. Land-locked countries, like Germany, found that they were excluded from participating in the lucrative new economy. On the other hand, those countries which bordered the Atlantic (England, France, Spain, and Portugal) were the most powerful players.

Literature and Science

Although the Renaissance is typically associated with achievements in visual art, the period also saw a magnificent outpouring of literary and scientific talent. One of the most significant works to emerge from this period was <u>The Prince</u>, by the Florentine Niccolo Macchiavelli. This book outlined a practical plan for political management, one that would be emulated by ruthless leaders in the future. Some of the other noteworthy authors were Erasmus (In Praise of Folly), Sir Thomas More (Utopia), Montaigne, Cervantes (Don Quixote), Ben Johnson, Christopher Marlowe, and, of course, William Shakespeare. At the same time, remarkable advances were being made in the sciences. Copernicus incited controversy by suggesting that the Earth revolved around the Sun; Kepler and Galileo would acquire hard data to support this claim.

Age of Exploration

Major European Explorers

Vasco da Gama was the first European to sail around the Cape of Good Hope, on the southern tip of what is now South Africa. This made it possible to reach Asia by boat. Balboa explored Central America, and was the first European to view the Pacific Ocean. Magellan is remembered as the first to circumnavigate the globe. Cortes was a powerful commander who subjugated the Aztecs in what is now Mexico; he used great brutality to achieve his ends. Pizarro, like Cortes, was a conquistador; he conquered the Incas in what is now Peru. Amerigo Vespucci, from whose name the word "America" was derived, mapped the Atlantic coast of South America and was able to convince stubborn Europeans that these lands were not a part of India.

Obstacles to Exploration

Before 1400, few Europeans knew anything about the world. When Christopher Columbus read of the exploits of the Italian Marco Polo, however, he was inspired to seek out new trade routes. Also, Prince Henry of Portugal established a navigation institute that encouraged sailors to explore. For a long time, extended sea voyages were restricted by a lack of navigational and seafaring technology; the inventions of the compass, astrolabe, and caravel remedied this situation. There was also a high cost associated with long travels; around 1400, however, new monarchs in France, England, Spain, and Portugal decided that they were willing to pay a high price to get a piece of the spice trade. Finally, the question of a motive for exploration was answered by the increasing fervor for missionary work, as well as the economic necessity of developing new trade routes.

Mercantilism

As foreign trade became the most important part of every nation's economy, the economic theory of mercantilism became popular. According to mercantilism, a nation should never import more than it exports. Of course, it is impossible for every country to achieve this goal at the same time, and so European countries were in fierce competition at all times. The solution that most nations pursued was to establish colonies, because these could supply resources for export by the mother country without really being considered imports. This rush to colonize had disastrous consequences for the indigenous peoples of the Americas and Africa. Europeans often looted the Native Americans for anything of value, and their need for cheap labor to cultivate the land there spawned the African slave trade.

Joint-Stock Companies

As exploration created new opportunities for amassing wealth, Portugal enjoyed special favor because of its excellent location and cordial relations with many of the Muslim nations of North Africa. The ruler of Portugal at this time was even known as Prince Henry "the Navigator" (1394-1460). In order to solidify trade arrangements, European rulers began to think about colonizing foreign lands. In order to fund these expensive trips, a new kind of business known as the joint-stock company was developed. In a joint-stock company, a group of merchants would combine their resources to pay for the passage of a vessel. These groups would later be influential in securing colonial charters for many of their agents. One of the most powerful examples was the Muscovy Company of England, which controlled almost all trade with Russia.

Cortez and His Relationship with the Aztecs

Hernán Cortez (1485-1547) was a Spanish conquistador. He assisted in the conquest of Cuba, and lived there until 1518, when he was assigned to lead an expedition into Mexico. He and 700 men landed on the Mexican shore and he promptly had his ships burnt, in order to indicate his sincerity about establishing a foothold in the country. Cortez then led his troops into Tenochtitlan, the capital of the Aztec Empire. They were received graciously by the Aztec ruler, Montezuma, whom they immediately enslaved. The Aztecs tried to revolt against the Spanish influence, but Cortez formed a coalition with other anti-Aztec groups and brutally eliminated the Aztec uprising. Cortez went on to rule "New Spain" for a number of years.

Pizarro and the Incas

Francisco Pizarro (c. 1478- 1541) was a Spanish explorer. He lived for a time in what is now Panama, where he heard tales of the fabulous wealth enjoyed by the Incas in the Andes Mountains. Pizarro determined to conquer this empire, and with 168 men he reached the Incan city of Tumbez in 1532. At this time, the Incas were in the middle of a civil war. Pizarro used this to his advantage: he massacred one side and took their leader prisoner. In order to free himself, the leader arranged a huge ransom, which Pizarro collected and then ignored, killing the leader anyway. Soon, Spaniards conquered the Incan city of Cuzco, and installed a puppet regime. After some turmoil, Pizarro took over the leadership of Peru until his assassination in 1541.

Reformation

A response to corruption in the Catholic Church and lapses in enforcement of the basic tenets of the faith, such as those against simony, the Reformation was a movement that called for a return to what many believed to be a simpler message of salvation that they felt to be more scripturally accurate. Many people in this time were outraged by the vast land holdings and stuffed coffers of the Church, which they felt should be concerned with tending to the spiritual health of its members. The invention of the printing press had made it possible for ideas to be disseminated more widely, and authors of the Renaissance had sharply criticized the greed of the clergy. People were also angered by the selling of ecclesial offices and especially the selling of indulgences, in which a person would pay money to have one's time in Purgatory shortened. Selling salvation was indeed against the tenets of the Church, but was often largely unenforced. The general distrust of the Church in this period is known as anticlericalism.

Martin Luther

Martin Luther was a German friar who first became famous for criticizing the Catholic Church's sale of indulgences. In accordance with the tradition of theological debate, Luther posted his critique of this practice on the door of his local church; the document known as the "Ninety-five Theses" won him immediate fame. Luther then set about undermining the institution of the Church, arguing that individuals did not need the help of clergy to establish a strong relationship with God. Luther went even further, stating that faith, rather than obedience to arbitrary Church rules, would be what got individuals into heaven. The final straw for the Church came when Luther directly challenged the Pope, declaring that no one man could be the perfect interpreter of Scripture. Luther was excommunicated, but continued to spread his message. Germany was then wracked by a war between the Lutherans of the north and the Catholics of the south. The Peace of Augsburg in 1555 was the resolution to this conflict, in which the subjects of a prince would follow that prince's faith, a practice referred to as "cuius regio, cuius religio"—literally, "whose jurisdiction, whose religion".

Counter-Reformation

After being bombarded by Protestant attacks for years, the Catholic Church finally began to make some positive changes. This program was known as the Counter-Reformation, and it was aimed at stopping the spread of Protestantism. For instance, the sale of indulgences was halted, and more authority was given to local bishops. The Church reaffirmed many of its core teachings (such as the earning of indulgences, transubstantiation, veneration of the Virgin Mary, the necessity of works, et cetera) yet admitted its errors with regard to simony and abuses of clerical power, which were quickly remedied. One of the most influential men of this movement was Sir Ignatius Loyola, a

Spaniard who founded the Society of Jesus (the Jesuits) to promote the Catholic interpretation of Scripture. The Council of Trent was a 20-year meeting that determined the official Catholic interpretation on all matters of theology. The Counter-Reformation also saw the reemergence of the Inquisition, in which heretics were sought out and punished.

Protestants

Inspired by Luther, many other critics of Catholic excess joined together throughout Europe. These groups were known collectively as Protestants. One of the largest sects of Protestants were the Calvinists, named after founder John Calvin. This group believed in the idea of predestination, or that God had already fixed each person's eternal destiny, and that only the Elect would join Him in heaven. Naturally, most people believed themselves to be among the Elect. In England, King Henry VIII split from the Catholic Church after his request for an annulment from Catherine of Aragon was denied by the Pope. Henry established the Church of England with himself as leader, and had five more wives before his death.

Era of European monarchies (1500-1650)

Between the years 1500 and 1650, most of the major European powers were led by absolute monarchs, who claimed a divine right to rule. These European monarchies often consolidated their power by marrying into one another. The strength of the monarchies fostered a resurgent spirit of nationalism, and consequently led to more frequent conflicts between nations. In 1500, Spain was probably the most powerful nation in Europe, because of her lucrative colonies and impressive Armada. Over the next century and a half, however, France and England would emerge as the dominant powers in the region. Germany and Russia, though largely excluded from shipping, were still powerful during this period.

Powers of Spain between 1500 and 1650

The height of Spanish power began with the reign of King Ferdinand and Queen Isabella; these monarchs promoted exploration and became fantastically rich as a result. The Hapsburg King Charles V would increase Spain's prominence and territory, because he had acquired lands in France, Austria, and Germany through inheritance. Spain was drawn into a number of conflicts over these new possessions, however: France disputed his claim to parts of Italy, and the Ottoman Turks challenged his Armada in the Mediterranean. Charles V would finally be forced to abdicate the throne, leaving his brother Ferdinand I in control of Austria and Germany, and his son Philip II in control of Spain and some western lands. During Philip's reign, most of these possessions would be lost; particularly bitter was the loss of the Netherlands, which quickly became a trading power in their own right.

Cromwell and William and Mary

The alliance of Parliament and the Puritans was led by Oliver Cromwell. His army was successful in deposing and executing King Charles I, and Cromwell was subsequently installed as Protector of England. Cromwell's rule was undermined by Anglican nobles and clergy who disliked his Puritanism. After the death of Cromwell, England was ruled by the two sons of Charles I, Charles II and James II, the latter of which was forced to abdicate by Parliament. After this period of relative chaos, William and Mary of the Netherlands were asked to rule England in a limited monarchy. This shift in power was known as the Glorious Revolution. The Declaration of Rights that limited the power of the monarchy gave Parliament more power, and made possible a long period of tranquility.

ENGLAND DURING THE TUDOR AND STUART RULINGS

For many years, England was ruled by the Tudor family. Henry VIII, the founder of the Anglican Church, had been a Tudor, and his daughter Elizabeth continued his policies. During the Elizabethan age in England, trading and exploration increased and the Spanish Armada, sent to overthrow Elizabeth as a protestant heretic, was defeated. After Elizabeth died in 1603, the Stuart family ascended to the throne. The Stuart period would be marked by conflict. Both James I and Charles I butted heads with Parliament over the issue of taxation, and there were also continual conflicts between Puritans (followers of John Calvin) and Anglicans (adherents of the Church of England). The Puritans joined with Parliament in opposition to the monarchy.

GOVERNMENT OF GERMANY BETWEEN 1500 AND 1650

Unlike many of the other Western European powers in 1500, Germany was still essentially just a collection of disjointed city-states. The Hapsburg family was powerful there, but the lands they called their Holy Roman Empire were not well organized, and the Hapsburgs were weak compared to other European leaders. The Peace of Augsburg, which had quelled disputes between Lutherans and Catholics, was destroyed by the Thirty Years' War (1618-48), which began when Protestants challenged the authority of the Hapsburg emperor. Germany would become so chaotic and disjointed during this period that other nations would step in, whether to seize some land or to help out one side or the other. The brutality of this war left Germany in a state of turmoil.

GOVERNMENT OF FRANCE BETWEEN 1500 AND 1650

While England was undergoing a turbulent transition from an absolute to a limited monarchy, France was governed by a succession of powerful and talented Bourbon monarchs. The Estates General, the French counterpart to the British Parliament, was not especially powerful. During a period in which the Bourbon heir was too young to govern himself, the charismatic Cardinal Richelieu governed France. Cardinal Richelieu was a Catholic, of course, but he did not persecute the French protestant Huguenot sect. Rather, he compromised with his enemies in an attempt to consolidate the power of the French crown. Cardinal Richelieu also established a strong bureaucracy, known as the noblesse de la robe.

GOVERNMENT OF RUSSIA BETWEEN 1500 AND 1650

As the nations of Western Europe were beginning to rely on foreign trade almost exclusively to support themselves, Russia remained a feudal nation. After the Mongols were overthrown, Russia was ruled by a succession of Czars, and Russia was largely excluded from the cultural rejuvenation of the Renaissance period. Instead, Russians suffered through the reign of Ivan the Terrible (1530-1584), a fierce ruler who pushed the borders out in the east with horrible brutality, and suffocated any rivals or critics. Ivan's reign was so oppressive that Russia could not develop a merchant class to rival those of the Western European powers, despite having some impressive natural resources.

Era of Global Wars

State Theory of Modernization vs. World System Theory of Modernization

The state theory of modernization supports the ideals of capitalism by maintaining that whenever the government is restricted from seizing private property, capitalism will develop and free markets will arise as people modernize and strive to become more productive. The world system theory of modernization, also known as the dependency theory, states that some nations modernize at the expense of less-developed nations, and that so long as this exploitation continues, the less-developed nations will be unable to improve their lot. This theory essentially takes the Marxist view of the capitalist society, in which those who own the means of production are able to maintain dominance over the workers, and applies it to the interactions of nations.

Globalization

Globalization is the process whereby all the social groups in the world are being brought into closer connection with one another. This has occurred mainly through the advances in transportation and communication technology, although the era of colonialism also had the effect of shrinking the world. This phenomenon has in some cases made it more difficult for repressive regimes to isolate themselves; during the Tiananmen Square uprising in China, for instance, Western media was able to communicate with the student rebels and present their story to the rest of the world. Many observers lament globalization, however, because they feel it will homogenize culture and crowd out fascinating, but not economically successful, societies.

World War I

Entangling Alliances Prior to WWI

In the early years of the twentieth century, relations among the various European powers were complex. Ever since the Franco-Prussian War, won by Prussia, the two sides had been enemies. At the center of their conflict was the territory of Alsace-Lorraine, which each side claimed as its own. In order to bolster their position in the region, each side entered into networks of alliances. After years of negotiations, two main alliances contained the major European powers: the Triple Alliance (Germany, Austria, Italy) and the Triple Entente (France, Britain, Russia). These two alliances would end up being the opposing sides in the great war of the ensuing years.

Early Combat During WWI and the Exit of Russia

Despite the fact that almost every nation in Europe had entered into World War I, most Europeans thought the conflict would be brief. Instead, advances in weapons technology made the war bloody and excruciatingly slow. Much of the fighting was done from trenches, and some battles would see the deaths of thousands of soldiers at a time. The war was also slow because the sides were very evenly matched; that is, until 1917, when the United States entered on the side of Britain. Also in 1917, the Russians exited the war via the Brest-Litovsk Treaty. Russia was basically exhausted after suffering through a Revolution in 1917 in which the Bolsheviks came to power. The entry of the US provided the British and French with supplies and troops, and Germany was soon forced to call for a truce.

Balkans and the Beginning of WWI

In the years before the First World War, the Balkans were attempting to gain independence from the Hapsburg empire of Austria. This insurrection culminated in the assassination of Austrian Archduke Franz Ferdinand in 1914 by Gavrilo Princip, a member of a Serbian nationalist group. At this point, a chain reaction of war declarations (spurred by the comprehensive alliances of the time) ensued. Austria declared war against Serbia; Germany and Turkey joined with the Austrians; Russia declared war on these countries in support of Serbia; France joined with Russia; and Britain and Italy joined forces with France, even though Italy had been a member of the Triple Alliance.

Russian Revolution of 1917

After the Revolution of 1905, Russia had enjoyed a few years of relative peace. After a while, however, the peasants became dissatisfied with the weakness of the Duma, and after strikes and protests Czar Nicholas II was forced to abdicate the throne. In place of the monarchy, a Provisional Government was set up to work alongside more progressive local councils, known as Soviets. These two groups were constantly at odds, however, especially during Russia's participation in the First World War (the Soviets wanted to withdraw and focus on national issues, while the Provisional Government felt obliged to fight). During this period, Vladimir Lenin rose to prominence as the Marxist leader of the Bolshevik Party. In the Russian Revolution of 1917, Lenin and his supporters ousted the Provisional Government and exited the War. Lenin then began the immense project of nationalizing the Soviet economy.

Treaty of Versailles

As the First World War wound down, a disgruntled German populace ousted the emperor and installed a moderate socialist government. This government, known as the Weimar Republic, would last until 1933. At the Paris Peace Conference, the victors of the war (the US, Britain, France, and Italy) exacted some revenge on Germany. The Treaty of Versailles penalized Germany economically and territorially: Alsace-Lorraine became independent, and the German military was dismantled. The Treaty of Versailles would need to be modified by two subsequent agreements: the Treaty of Locarno which outlined a more reasonable reparations plan for Germany, and the Kellogg-Briand Pact which asserted that diplomacy rather than force would be used to resolve conflicts.

Lenin and Stalin

After his success in the Revolution of 1917, Lenin began to advocate the revolt of the working class in other nations. Naturally, this did not endear the new Russian government to the leaders of other nations. Russia became increasingly isolated both economically and politically from the rest of the world. Domestically, Lenin established the New Economic Policy, which blended capitalism and communism. This plan worked well enough in agriculture, but it never achieved much success in industry. After Lenin's death, Joseph Stalin came to power and began an ambitious plan of collectivizing farms and nationalizing factories (known as the Five Year Plans). Stalin was ruthless in the pursuit of his goals; he established labor camps to house his opponents. It is estimated that 20 million people were killed by Stalin's regime during the period now known as the Great Terror.

Western Europe and Italy after the First World War

In the years after the First World War, the general mood in Europe was one of wariness. Most nations were exhausted by the conflict, and few felt that the signing of the Treaty of Versailles and the formation of the League of Nations had created a permanent peace. In the 1920s, Britain, Germany, France, and the United States were all liberal democracies without a strong executive. Unlike the United States, however, even the victorious European nations suffered a profound economic depression. One nation that saw no diminution in nationalism was Italy. In part out of a fear of communism, Italians supported the rise of the fascist dictator Benito Mussolini. Fascism was a political philosophy that promised Italians a return to the glory days of Rome, when they were a mighty power ruled by a dominating executive. Of course, in order to maintain his authority Mussolini had to brutally suppress any opposition.

China in the Early Twentieth Century

In 1911, the Manchu dynasty, which had been significantly weakened by the Boxer Rebellion, was finally overthrown. A period of instability followed, in which Sun Yat-sen declared the creation of a republic with its headquarters in Nanking. Sun Yat-sen began a political party aimed at improving life for the common people; it was known as the Kuomintang. During this period, both Mongolia and Tibet declared their independence from China. The Chinese people became disenchanted with the Kuomintang government after what they saw as unfavorable agreements following World War 1. After the death of Sun Yat-sen in 1925, a national government was established at Canton; the communist party was a major participant in this government.

Sino-Japanese War in 20th Century China

In 1926, the military leader Chiang Kai-shek led campaigns in central and northern China, in the hopes of unifying the country. During this period, Chiang broke with the communist party, and Communists were persecuted in Shanghai. In 1927, a national government led by the Kuomintang, who had previously fallen out of favor, was established in Nanking. The peasants were not pleased with this leadership, and they were organized as the Red Army under Mao Tse-tung in the south. In what is known as the Long March, Mao led his army north to Yenan, where they would gather strength. The situation in China was made even more volatile by the Japanese invasion in 1937. In what is known as the "Rape of Nanking," Japanese troops killed over 200,000 Chinese. The people were outraged, and the partisan splits between Mao's communists and Chiang's government only widened.

Japan in the Years Before WWII

In 1926, amid growing nationalism, Hirohito became the Emperor of Japan. The next year, the Japanese prime minister declared that Japan should dominate Asia, and four years later Japanese forces invaded Manchuria. Some historians consider this to be the beginning of the Second World War. After establishing a puppet regime in Manchuria, the Japanese withdrew from the League of Nations and attacked China. The Sino-Japanese War ensued. In 1938, Japan outlined its new vision of Co-prosperity Spheres: Japan would be the industrial center of Asia, and would acquire its raw materials from its colonies in the rest of Asia. Japan promoted this idea as an opportunity to break from European imperialism, but it was really just the substitution of one master for another. In 1940, Japan would complete its transformation into a fascist state by dissolving all political parties.

World War II

Events Leading Up to World War II

Still shell-shocked from the First World War, the nations of western Europe were slow to respond to the growing menace of Nazi Germany. In general, they pursued a policy of appeasement and isolation. The British prime minister Neville Chamberlain was especially committed to using diplomacy over war. Then, in 1936, Hitler sent troops to occupy the Rhineland, a strip of territory on the German border. At around the same time, Mussolini invaded Ethiopia; the two aggressors, Germany and Italy, entered into an agreement making them the Axis Powers. In 1938, Germany annexed Austria and indicated that it was about to attack Czechoslovakia. In response to these actions, Chamberlain brought together Mussolini and Hitler for the Munich Conference of 1938. These talks would only briefly suspend German aggression.

Weimar Republic and the Rise of Hitler

After the abdication of the emperor, Germany was ruled by a legislative body known as the Weimar Republic. Most Germans felt that this group had been too willing to accept punishment in the treaties that followed the war. Germans also thought that this government was responsible for the inflation which crippled the German economy in the post-war period. Germany, then, was vulnerable to the charms of a leader who told them they had nothing about which to be ashamed. This leader was Adolf Hitler (1889-1945). A failed artist, Hitler became the head of the National Socialist, or Nazi, party. His speeches were expressions of ardent nationalism, although often Hitler seemed to be calling for a return to an ideal German state that had never actually existed.

BELIEF SYSTEM OF THE NAZI PARTY

Led by Adolf Hitler, the Nazi party championed the Aryan race as superior to all others, especially the "insidious" Jews. Hitler suggested that the noble ambitions of the true German people required lebensraum, or living space. In other words, Germany needed more territory. In its early days, the Nazi party was part of the German republican system; Nazi candidates ran for office and served in the Reichstag (German parliament). As Germany suffered through a terrible economic depression in the early 1930s, however, the people became impatient. In 1933, the Reichstag "accidentally" caught on fire and the Nazis used the opportunity to claim total control of the government. Hitler was named Chancellor of Germany. He was able to quickly improve the German economy, mostly through the expansion of the weapon-building industry. At the same time, the new government began to quietly round up Jews, Gypsies, and homosexuals.

CONSEQUENCES OF THE HOLOCAUST

Many of the Nazi leaders were tried and convicted at the Nuremberg trials for their roles in the Holocaust. West Germany would later issue a Federal Compensation Law, through which billions of dollars were paid to survivors. During and after the Holocaust, Zionist Jews fled to Palestine. Public sympathy with their plight would be a main reason for the creation of Israel in 1948. The total destruction of the Jewish community in Europe caused many Jews to question their faith, and those that remained in Europe are markedly more secular than their ancestors. The shock of the Holocaust has also caused many institutions, including the Roman Catholic Church, to consider their own latent anti-Semitism. Unfortunately, the anti-genocide legislation created in response to the Holocaust was not strict enough to rally international support against the Rwandans (who slaughtered hundred of thousands of Tutsis in 1994), or the Bosnian Serbs and Croats (who killed thousands of Muslims in the early 1990s).

OVERVIEW OF THE HOLOCAUST

The Holocaust is the name given to the systematic killing of Jews, gypsies, homosexuals, and others by the Nazis. Anti-Semitism had existed in Europe for millennia, but the Nazis gave it renewed emphasis, and after making numerous false claims about Jews, began persecuting them upon Hitler's rise to power in 1933. Jews were disenfranchised, forced into ghettos, had their property taken, and were finally sent to work and be killed in concentration camps. Approximately 6 million Jews were killed during the Holocaust. As the situation for the Germans became more dire in the Second World War, Hitler sought to implement what he called the "final solution," in which hundreds of thousands were killed just before the fall of Nazi Germany.

BEGINNING AND INITIAL YEARS OF WORLD WAR II

After Chamberlain had tried to forestall German aggression at the Munich Conference of 1938, Germany nevertheless invaded Czechoslovakia in 1939. It was also during this year that Hitler signed a secret agreement with Stalin pledging not to attack Russia so long as Russia stayed out of German affairs. Hitler then declared war on and conquered Poland. At this step, Great Britain and France were finally forced to declare war upon Germany. Germany at this point was a dominating military adversary. New advances in motorized military vehicles made it possible for Germany to conquer large areas of land quickly in a new form of warfare called Blitzkrieg (lightning-war). The Axis powers conquered almost the entire European continent, including France, over the course of

1940. Only Great Britain remained in opposition, and the Nazis undertook a ferocious aerial assault on the British, who were by then led by Winston Churchill, but failed to do enough damage to make an invasion of the island country practical. Instead, Hitler turned East and decided to violate his truce with Stalin, invading Russia in 1941 and overwhelming much of the Soviet military and advancing deep into Russian territory in a huge surprise offensive.

Middle Years and Conclusion of World War II

The tide turned against Hitler once the United States entered the war. The harsh Russian winter halted the German advance into Russia short of Moscow in 1941. The Germans made further gains in the summer of 1942, but were decisively beaten at the battle of Stalingrad and were slowly pushed back out of Russia from then on. American and British troops landed in North Africa in 1942 and used that as a springboard to invade Italy in 1943. In 1944, the Americans and British opened yet another front with a massive invasion of northern France in the D-Day landings. Fighting numerically superior forces on multiple fronts, the Germans steadily lost ground and the Allies pushed into Germany from both East and West in 1945. Surrounded and with the war lost, Hitler commited suicide in his bunker in Berlin in April, 1945 and the remaining German forces surrendered shortly afterwards.

Pacific Arena in WWII

The Japanese, like the Germans, became seduced by the notion of their own racial superiority during the 1930s. As in Germany, this inevitably led to a lust for territorial expansion. By 1941, Japan had conquered Korea, Manchuria, and parts of China. Japan was also threatening to invade American interests in the Philipines. The United States imposed economic sanctions on Japan making it difficult for the Japanese war industry to function. In response, the Japanese launched a surprise attack on the United States by bombing the US naval base of Pearl Harbor. After the attack on Pearl Harbor, the United States would declare war upon Japan (and Germany would in turn declare war on the United States). The Japanese made huge territorial gains before the US turned the tide at the Battles of Midway and Guadalcanal. The war in the Pacific would take much longer than the war in Europe due to the island hopping nature of the fight. The Japanese unwillingness to surrender made it almost impossible for America to entirely vanquish them without enormous lose of life. So the United States decided to drop atomic bombs on Hiroshima and Nagasaki to force Japan to surrender and finally end the war in the Pacific in August 1945.

The Post War Period

Communist Revolution in China

China was torn by civil strife all throughout the Second World War. At one point, the American government had to renounce its trade rights in China in order to persuade China not to sign a peace treaty with Japan while the US still needed Chinese support. Once Japan had been defeated, the Red Army under Mao moved into Manchuria (which had recently been vacated by the Soviets). The major cities were still occupied by Nationalist forces, supported by the Americans. In 1946, fighting resumed between the opposing factions, and the Nationalists under Chiang were eventually forced to abandon central China. In 1949, the Red Army forced Chiang Kai-shek to leave the mainland and find refuge on Taiwan. On October 1, 1949, the communists declared the official creation of the People's Republic of China.

The Cold War

Beginnings of The Cold War

After the defeat of the Axis powers in WWII, the United States and Russia entered into a long and often secret conflict, in which each side used diplomatic, economic, and occasionally military forces to try to assert itself as the dominant world power. The first issue on which these nations butted heads was the rebuilding of Europe. Germany was divided into an eastern and western section; the western half was democratic and looked to the US for guidance, while Eastern Germany became a communist nation in the USSR's sphere of influence. Russia worked to bring all of its neighbors (including Poland, Czechoslovakia, Hungary, Romania, and Bulgaria) under its control. The western borders of these nations formed what Churchill referred to as the iron curtain, dividing communist Eastern Europe from democratic Western Europe.

In order to stop the spread of communism in Europe and elsewhere, the President Truman asserted his policy of "containment" in the so-called *Truman Doctrine*. This meant that the US would support the anticommunist governments throughout the world. The *Marshall Plan* advanced this policy by supplying aid to war-ravaged countries in Western Europe. When the Eastern Bloc countries prevented aid from reaching West Berlin, the US , England, and France organized the Berlin Airlift to overcome this obstacle. In 1949, the Western European and North American nations entered into a mutual defense treaty, *NATO* (North Atlantic Treaty Organization). As a response, the eastern Bloc nations joined with the Soviet Union in the *Warsaw Pact.*

During the Cold War, the United States and the Soviet Union each tried to deter an attack by the other by building up fantastic arsenals of nuclear missiles. The two nations would also expend considerable effort trying to be the first in space. Finally, in the late 60s and early 70s, the two nations would begin talks aimed at mutual disarmament. This occurred in part because relations between China and the USSR had cooled. Before this period of détente, however, there had been a couple of serious threats to global peace. In 1961, the US had financed an unsuccessful invasion of Cuba at the Bay of Pigs. This led the Soviet Union to establish missile bases on communist Cuba; the US and USSR almost declared war on one another during the Cuban Missile Crisis of 1962.

End of the Cold War

Over time, the leaders of the Soviet Union and United States began to realize the total annihilation that would ensue if nuclear war was declared, and it was agreed that both sides would disarm. The two treaties that were signed during the 1970s are known as the Strategic Arms Limitation Talks (SALT) I and II. When Mikhail Gorbachev came into power in the USSR in 1985, he established a policy of glasnost, or "openness." In response to US President Ronald Reagan's military build-up using the might of the US economy, Gorbachev understood that the Soviet Union could not economically compete militarily under a communist system and overcome the military might of the United States. He thus advocated perestroika, a gradual metamorphosis of the Soviet economy. In 1991, these reforms culminated in the disintegration of the ruling Communist party, and the disbanding of the Soviet Union. This occurred two years after the Berlin Wall, which for more than forty years had separated communist and anticommunist Germany, was finally torn down.

MIDDLE EAST

MIDDLE EAST FROM 1947 TO 1977

After WWII, the United Nations announced that Palestine would be partitioned in order to make room for a new Jewish state. Israel was created in 1948. In 1951, the Iranian leader Mossadegh nationalized the oil interests, making his government extremely wealthy and powerful. This move would be emulated by future leaders. In 1967, in the Six Day War, Israel routed a coalition of Arab nations, seizing the West Bank, Sinai, and Jerusalem. In 1972, Palestinian terrorists murdered 12 Israeli athletes at the Olympics in Munich. In 1973, the oil-producing Arab nations placed an embargo on shipments to the West, causing major energy crises in the US and Europe. Also in 1973, Israelis and Arabs battled again in the Yom Kippur War. In 1977, Egyptian leader Anwar Sadat became the first Arab leader to visit Israel.

MIDDLE EAST FROM 1978 TO 1985

In 1978, American President Jimmy Carter hosted successful peace talks between Egypt and Israel at Camp David. The next year, however, a fundamentalist Islamist regime would take power in Iran, and many Americans would be taken hostage, only released upon the election of Ronald Reagan. Between 1980 and 1988, Iran and Iraq engaged in a bloody and brutal war, begun when the Iraqi leader Saddam Hussein seized territory in eastern Iran. Also during this period, Afghan rebels were engaged in a prolonged, ultimately successful fight for independence from the Soviets. In 1982, Israel attacked Lebanon, which was harboring the Palestinian leader Yasser Arafat. Lebanon would be forced to oust Arafat the next year. Israel would continue attacking Arafat and the Palestinian Liberation Organization, and the PLO would continue to sponsor terrorist activities against Israel.

MIDDLE EAST FROM 1987 TO 2003

In 1987, Syrian troops entered Lebanon and stopped the civil war. Also during this year, 402 pilgrims died during riots in the Saudi Arabian sacred city of Mecca. In 1988, the Palestinian resistance (known as the Intifada) began in earnest against Israel. Iraq invaded Kuwait in 1990, and after UN sanctions were levied, the US invaded in 1991. The Iraqi soldiers set fire to thousands of Kuwaiti oil wells while retreating. In 1992, Arafat and Israeli PM Yitzhak Rabin shook hands in Washington and Arafat would soon return to Gaza after years of exile. In 1995, the Israelis and Palestinians signed an agreement giving the Palestinians autonomy in the West Bank and Gaza areas. Despite continuing violence, another agreement was reached in 1998, this one stating that the Palestinians would be granted land in exchange for keeping the peace. Violence continued, however, and in 2003 Israel began construction of a barrier between itself and the Palestinian territories.

INDIA AND PAKISTAN AFTER WWII

In 1947, after years of peaceful protests led by Mahatma Gandhi, India was given its independence and partitioned into two states, India and Pakistan. The following year, Gandhi would be assassinated in India. In 1965, border disputes would flare into the Indo-Pakistani War. In 1971, Pakistan would fend off attacks from Bengali rebels, who sought to achieve independence. The next year, however, Bangladesh would be established as an independent state. In 1984, India had its own internal problems: after the Indian army occupied the Golden Temple sacred to the Sikhs, the Indian leader Indira Gandhi was assassinated by her Sikh bodyguards. Anti-Sikh riots resulted, and much blood was shed.

NEW EUROPE

1991 THROUGH 1998

In 1991, Gorbachev resigned as the last president of the USSR, and a number of the Soviet provinces, including Lithuania and Latvia, declared independence. The Maastricht Treaty, formally announcing the creation of the European Union, was signed in 1992, and the next year a unified European stock market opened. In the "Velvet" Revolution of 1993, Slovakia separated from Czechoslovakia, which became the Czech Republic. Meanwhile, the former USSR was enduring civil strife until Boris Yeltsin seized power in 1993. In 1994, Russian troops attacked Chechnya, which was trying to achieve independence. In 1998, President Clinton helped broker a peace agreement between the British and North Irish rebels.

AFTER 1999

In 1999, the Czech Republic, Poland, and Hungary all joined NATO, further eliminating the old divides between western and eastern Europe. The conflict in Chechnya increased during this year, and Yeltsin was succeeded as Russian leader by the former KGB agent Vladimir Putin. An International Criminal Court was created in the Hague (Netherlands) in 2002, despite the vehement opposition of the United States. In the late nineties, many of the western European governments had become quasi-socialist, and they spent much of their time debating the immense increase in immigration. Meanwhile, the former Soviet states have had a rough transition from command to market economies, and are still somewhat economically depressed.

PACIFIC RIM AFTER 1991

In the 1990's and early years of the 21st century, Japan and China have emerged as two major economic powers. Despite suffering a prolonged recession, Japan continued to be one of the world's manufacturing leaders. However, several internal scandals have shaken Japanese confidence and caused many to question the close relations between corporations and government. In China, the suffocating communist regime has relaxed its economic strictures somewhat, and the result has been an economic boom. China created several Special Economic Zones along its eastern coast to lure foreign business; at present, however, Chinese firms are beginning to control a sizable portion of the market in their own right.

FIRST WORLD, SECOND WORLD AND THIRD WORLD

First World nations are those that have advanced capitalist economies and are fully industrialized. The former Soviet states, which are slowly developing capitalist economies after having inefficient socialist economies for so long, are classified as *Second World* nations. This term has fallen out of general use, as these nations have slowly become more similar to First World nations. The relatively poor and nonindustrialised nations of Latin America, Africa, and Asia, most of which were colonized or involved in other exploitative trade arrangements with the Western empires at one time, are known as the *Third World* nations. Although these nations are far more numerous than those of the First or Second World, they wield much less political power.

MODERNIZATION

Modernization is the process by which societies develop sophisticated industrial technology, as well as the political, cultural, and social systems that are most effective in sustaining and advancing that technology. For a long time, historians have noted that the most modernized countries, namely the Western empires, were the most successful, and that other societies should strive to emulate them.

In recent decades, however, more sensitive sociologists have declared that modernization need not be equated with Westernization, and that the indigenous cultures of South America and Africa, for example, need not be cast off for these places to enjoy prosperity. One way sociologists can assess the relative modernization of a society is by comparing the gross national product: the total value of all economic activity within a society. Often, GNP is divided by total population to determine a society's per capita gross national product.

Automation

Automation is when machines are employed to do work formerly done by humans. This is typically done when an industry seeks to have greater worker productivity, but it may have some costly side effects. The work that remains for people after automation is frequently repetitive and mindless. Historians studying the phenomenon have observed increased alienation and lowered self-esteem among workers whose jobs have been automated. Also, automation reduces the need for specialization by driving employees out of their previously unique fields; this creates both unhealthy competition for menial jobs, and confusion over social roles among the workers. Unfortunately, the pressures of the capitalist market make it impossible for most businesses to avoid automation.

Hyper-Urbanization

Hyper-urbanization has occurred when the development of population growth in urban areas has moved too quickly and has outpaced the necessary accompanying growths in industry and business. The inevitable result of hyper-urbanization is unemployment and inadequate public services. This has been a particular problem in Third World countries, which are experiencing mass internal migration from the countryside to the cities. In fact, the urbanization currently taking place in China may be the largest movement of people in the history of the world. It is impossible for any society, not matter how wealthy, to keep up with such a migration and provide adequate roads, health care, education, water, food and electricity.

Underdevelopment

Third World countries that do not have the modern economic conditions possessed by the wealthier nations are said to suffer from underdevelopment. That is, they do not have the industrial, social, or political strength that is required to be a self-sustaining party in the global economy. In some countries, underdevelopment is clearly the result of dysfunctional politics: Third World nations are more likely to be ruled by a small group or by a dictator. Underdeveloped nations are typically those that were colonized at one time. Because their economy during the colonial period was so heavily based upon exporting raw materials, they never created a manufacturing base and found themselves unequipped for independence. Experts are at odds as to whether First World nations should aid underdeveloped countries by funneling money to them or by helping them to develop modern economies.

Technological Advances Since 1991

In 1993, the first web browser was developed, beginning the era of internet communications that has revolutionized every area of human life. The Internet did not become widely used, however, until 1997 and 1998. In 1997, a Scottish lab successfully cloned a lamb from adult sheep DNA, opening the door to the cloning of other animals, or human organs for medical purposes, and even for the cloning of entire human beings. This last possibility was strengthened in 2001, when the work of sequencing the DNA of the human genome was finally finished. Although embryonic stem-cell research has been limited in the US (other sources than embryos remain legal), other countries are using cells from human embryos to search for cures for disease.

Practice Test

Practice Questions

1. What is true about Martin Luther's 95 Theses?

a. Luther was opposed to the Church's sales of indulgences
b. Luther believed in practicing simony to support churches
c. Luther felt that clerical celibacy should be better enforced
d. Luther supported the majority of the church's sacraments

2. Which of the following is correct relative to the Protestant Reformation in Europe?

a. The end of the Thirty Years' War triggered the Protestant Reformation
b. The Protestant work ethic was credited with capitalism and prosperity
c. The Treaty of Westphalia impeded the development of Protestantism
d. The Treaty of Westphalia reinforced the political authority of the Pope

3. In the second era of the Atlantic system of slave trade, when were the largest proportion of African slaves bought by Europeans?

a. 1450–1600
b. The 1600s
c. The 1700s
d. The 1800s

4. Which of the following is the best example of a factor resulting from Europe's Commercial Revolution that contributed to the 1700s' Industrial Revolution?

a. The rediscovery of concrete
b. New advances in making iron
c. The steam engine's invention
d. Increases in population growth

5. In the 18th and 19th centuries, the Industrial Revolution eventually spread worldwide after beginning in which area?

a. North America
b. Great Britain
c. Germany
d. France

6. Which of the following is true of social changes and the Industrial Revolution in Europe in the 18th and early 19th centuries?

a. They gave rise to a new middle class
b. They improved working conditions
c. They were the result of urbanization
d. They were caused by the labor unions

7. What is correct regarding the movement known as the Enlightenment?

a. It emphasized faith above rationalism
b. It influenced the American Revolution
c. It was caused by the French Revolution
d. It had no effect on Poland or Lithuania

8. In general, which of the following went down, NOT up, until the end of the 19th century due to the Industrial Revolution?

a. Population growth
b. Public literacy
c. Standards of living
d. Workers' earnings

9. Regarding the Industrial Revolution's transition from mercantilism to capitalism, which of these economists both refuted mercantilist concepts of finite wealth and advocated free trade?

a. David Ricardo
b. David Hume
c. Both A and D
d. Adam Smith

10. Which of the following is most true about European imperialism on other continents?

a. Colonization did not begin until during the 19th century
b. It began in the 15th century, increasing greatly in the 19th
c. It started in the 17th century and escalated during the 18th
d. Colonization overseas was most active in the 16th century

11. Of the following Enlightenment proponents of social contract theory, which one advocated absolute monarchy?

a. Jean-Jacques Rousseau
b. Pierre-Joseph Proudhon
c. Thomas Hobbes
d. John Locke

12. What is correct regarding European imperialism abroad between 1400 and 1900?

a. England was the country to colonize the most places
b. England was the earliest to colonize countries abroad
c. England was the one that kept some colonies longest
d. England was dominant in Southeast Asia and North Africa

13. In the last decades of the 19th century, which countries competed for control of Africa?

a. England and France
b. England, France, and Germany
c. England, France, Germany, and Italy
d. England, France, Germany, Italy, and Belgium

14. Which of these was true of African countries and their European colonization by the end of the 19th century?

a. Ethiopia and Liberia were fully unoccupied by Europeans
b. This was not the period with Sudan's brief independence
c. Every country in Africa was a European colony at this time
d. Only Mali, Malawi, and Nigeria were independent states

15. Where do historians consider the Enlightenment to have first begun?

a. Britain
b. France
c. America
d. Germany

16. During World War I, which group joined with the Central Powers after it formed?

a. Austria-Hungary
b. Germany
c. Ottoman Empire
d. Italy

17. While many events contributed, which group committed the action that finally triggered the start of World War I?

a. German nationals
b. Austrian nationals
c. Bosnian nationals
d. Serbian nationals

18. What is true about the beginning of World War II?

a. Hitler's attack on Poland violated his previous agreement
b. Germany was issued an ultimatum by Britain and America
c. The Soviet Union had invaded Poland before Germany did
d. The Soviet Union attacked Germany two years after Poland

19. Which of the following is correct about the Cold War period?

a. World War II's adversarial relationship of the USSR and USA continued
b. The Marshall Plan was implemented aiming to contain Communism
c. The United States formed NATO to be a defensive military alliance
d. The Truman Doctrine was designed to help rebuild postwar Europe

20. Which of the following statements about events following the end of World War II is false?

a. The Cold War, including the nuclear arms race, lasted for over 40 years
b. Animosity and uncertainty gave rise to Fascism in Italy, Spain, and Germany
c. Though the United States bombed Japan to end the war, the two later became allies
d. Most European holdings in Asia and Africa were decolonized and freed

21. Which is one geographical reason that so many European immigrants settled in New York City?

a. The site of New York City was free of any natural barriers
b. The site of New York City was free of trees to be cleared
c. The site of New York City did not have a coastal location
d. The site of New York City had abundant water supplies

22. Which statement is true regarding the Suez and Panama canals?

a. Ferdinand de Lesseps led and completed both projects
b. The Panama Canal is twice the length of the Suez Canal
c. It was harder to construct the Panama Canal than the Suez
d. The Suez Canal was officially opened after the Panama

23. What is true about Queen Elizabeth I of England and Ireland?

a. Her governance was stricter than her father's, brother's, or sister's
b. She founded a Protestant Church that became the Church of England
c. The famed defeat of the Spanish Armada occurred outside her reign
d. Elizabeth had a number of courtships and was married several times

24. Which of the following is accurate regarding England's Queen Victoria?

a. England became a constitutional monarchy after her reign
b. During her reign, the British Empire diminished somewhat
c. She ruled longer than any other female monarch in history
d. She ascended to the throne in her teens and never married

25. What is true about the English Bill of Rights?

a. It was first ratified during the 18th century
b. It made it legal for Church courts to exist
c. It restored the Protestant right to bear arms
d. It allowed royals to levy taxes and judge

26. Which of the following is accurate regarding the United States Bill of Rights?

a. It is a separate document from Constitutional amendments
b. It gives the United States federal government more power
c. It was written and offered to Congress by Thomas Jefferson
d. It was adopted by the House in 1789 and was ratified by 1791

27. Of the following, which did France's Declaration of the Rights of Man and of the Citizen (1789) omit specifically addressing?

a. The matter of slavery
b. The rights of women
c. The right to property
d. Both answers A and B

28. Which is correct regarding the Federal Convention that drafted the U.S. Constitution?

a. Its original purpose was to revise the Articles of Confederation
b. The power of central government was not an issue to members
c. Drafters were unconcerned with Congressional representation
d. Popular versus state elections were debated at another convention

29. What is true about the League of Nations?

a. The League followed a series of international peacekeeping organizations
b. President Wilson got a Nobel Peace Prize for advocating U.S. membership
c. The United States joined the League of Nations and ratified its Covenant
d. The League of Nations ultimately achieved its mission of preventing war

30. Which of the following is considered more a cause than an effect of the Industrial Revolution?

a. Emergence of socialism
b. Emergence of capitalism
c. The Romantic movement
d. The Protestant work ethic

31. What is accurate regarding Adam Smith's The Wealth of Nations?

a. There is evidence it influenced government soon after publication
b. The book and its author were uniformly lauded by English radicals
c. It was quoted by those arguing in favor of wars with other nations
d. It was quoted as supporting documentation in favor of slave trade

32. Who was the first recipient of two Nobel Prizes in two different fields?

a. Linus Pauling
b. Marie S. Curie
c. Albert Einstein
d. Thomas Edison

33. Which of the following is true about Louis Pasteur?

a. The first rabies vaccine was made by other scientists
b. The first anthrax vaccine was not in his contributions
c. His experiments refuted the germ theory of disease
d. He developed a process for reducing pathogens in food

34. Which group led the Counterreformation in response to the Protestant Reformation?

a. Anglicans
b. Lutherans
c. The Jesuits
d. Reformed

35. What is accurate regarding the beliefs of Martin Luther and other Protestant Reformers?

a. They opposed many Catholic doctrines but not papal authority
b. They questioned Catholic beliefs about the roles of the saints
c. They had no issues around the doctrine of particular judgment
d. They at least agreed with Catholic attitudes on the Virgin Mary

36. According to Martin Luther's own writing, which did he regard as the most central issue of the Protestant Reformation?

a. The Catholic church's sale of indulgences
b. The Catholic church's belief in purgatory
c. The Catholic doctrine of freedom of will
d. The Catholic Pope's degree of authority

37. Which of the following ancient civilizations of the Americas lived in Central America?

a. The Incas
b. The Aztecs
c. All of these
d. The Mayans

38. Of the following Pre-Columbian American civilizations, which one has descendants still living today?

a. The Mayans
b. The Aztecs
c. The Incas
d. None

39. Which is the earliest of the following civilizations to be destroyed by Spanish conquistadores?

a. The Mayans
b. The Aztecs
c. The Incas
d. A and B

40. Prior to the Atlantic slave trade, which was true about the practice of slavery in the world?

a. Slavery was practiced in Asia and Africa but not in Europe and the Americas
b. Slavery was practiced in Asia, Africa, and Europe but not in the Americas
c. Slavery was practiced already in Asia, Africa, Europe, and the Americas
d. Slavery was practiced in Europe, the Americas, and Africa but not Asia

41. Which of the following occurred latest in time and was one of the hallmarks of the Industrial Revolution in the 1700s?

a. Vasco da Gama opened a new trade route
b. International competition spurred colonization
c. Banking, stock, and insurance activity developed
d. James Watt invented the steam-powered engine

42. Which industry most proliferated through the Industrial Revolution's mechanization?

a. The textile industry
b. The cottage industry
c. The concrete industry
d. The watermill industry

43. Relative to trade unions and labor laws, which of these was chronologically latest in England?

a. The law that had made trade unions illegal was repealed
b. The law legalizing trade unions and their activities passed
c. The Ten Hours Act limited work hours for women and youth
d. The first Factory Act banned factory work for children under 9

44. Which of these is true about the movement of the Enlightenment?

a. New leaders' positions took precedence over public opinion
b. Empirical scientific methods were rejected in favor of beliefs
c. Its ideals differed drastically from modern Western culture's
d. Reason and knowledge were seen as ways to reform society

45. Which of these statements is most correct regarding effects of the Industrial Revolution?

a. Most citizens were too busy working in factories to care about politics
b. The Luddites, formed in reaction to industrialization, aided public political action
c. Industrialization raised public literacy, increasing political involvement
d. Industrialization led workers to disregard politics in favor of capitalism

46. The factory system developed in the Industrial Revolution made commodities of not only products, but also of what else?

a. Land
b. Labor
c. Money
d. All these

47. Which overseas location did Europeans colonize the earliest in time?

a. Latin America
b. Seaports in Asia
c. Seaports in Africa
d. Continental Africa

48. Of the following persons important to the Enlightenment, who was known for creating a means of spreading its ideas even more than having inspired them?

a. John Locke
b. Denis Diderot
c. Baruch Spinoza
d. Sir Isaac Newton

49. Of the following Enlightenment philosophers, who were proponents of social contract theory, whose version of the social contract was reflected in the U.S. Declaration of Independence?

a. Jean-Jacques Rousseau's
b. Thomas Hobbes's
c. David Hume's
d. John Locke's

50. Which of the following is true about European imperialism abroad between 1400 and 1900?

a. Germany and Italy began colonizing around the same time as England and France
b. England and France were the biggest in colonizing and also for the longest times
c. Holland, Portugal, and Spain colonized first and kept some colonies the longest
d. Dutch Boers settled in Africa before Spaniards conquered Latin American areas

51. In the late 19th century, which country officially owned what was probably Africa's most valuable asset, the Nile River?

a. Egypt
b. Africa
c. England
d. Belgium

52. Which of the following is true regarding the Enlightenment?

a. It developed as an opposite reaction to Romanticism
b. There was no such thing as a Counter-Enlightenment
c. No European monarchs ever accepted any of its ideas
d. German government was less hostile to it than French

53. In events surrounding World War I, which nation switched its allegiance from the Triple Alliance to the Triple Entente in 1915 and 1916?

a. Italy
b. Russia
c. France
d. Germany

54. At the beginning of World War I, which country did Germany wage war against first?

a. Serbia
b. Russia
c. France
d. Belgium

55. What is correct regarding American and Japanese involvement in World War II?

a. The Japanese declared war on America; then America declared war on Japan
b. The USA demanded Japan surrender after bombing Hiroshima and Nagasaki
c. America gave up its neutral isolationist policy after the attack on Pearl Harbor
d. America, Germany, and Italy declared war on one another at different times

56. Which of the following events did NOT take place during the Cold War period?

a. The Berlin Airlift
b. The Korean War
c. The Vietnam War
d. All of these

57. Which of these statements about events occurring in the late 19th to early 20th centuries is false?

a. The separation of church and state became official in France
b. England kept its isolationist policy toward continental Europe
c. England fell behind Germany and the United States in industrial production
d. Russia's Pan-Slavic policy caused conflicts between empires

58. Which geographic features were most conducive to the development of early civilizations?

a. Rivers
b. Deserts
c. Forests
d. Mountains

59. Which statement is true regarding the Suez Canal and the Panama Canal?

a. Only one of them is among the most important canals in the world
b. Both canals took much manual labor and were equally hard to build
c. One thing they have in common is political controversy over control
d. Both canals were constructed under similar geographical conditions

60. Which of the following world religions is the oldest?

a. Greek Stoicism
b. Confucianism
c. Christianity
d. Judaism

61. Of the following, which religion has the most followers?

a. Islam
b. Hinduism
c. Buddhism
d. Christianity

62. Which of the following was a hallmark of the reign of Elizabeth I?

a. An absence of overseas exploration
b. Strongly aggressive foreign relations
c. Famous achievements by dramatists
d. A lack of stability or national identity

63. Which of these is true about the reign of Queen Victoria?

a. She survived only one known assassination attempt while she was queen
b. Her Conservative and Liberal Prime Ministers' terms were equal in number
c. She gave much financial support to Ireland, contrary to some popular myths
d. During her reign, British foreign relations with France became much worse

64. The English Bill of Rights is known to have influenced the Canadian Charter of Rights and Freedoms. Which of these did it NOT also influence?

a. The United States of America's Bill of Rights
b. The European Convention on Human Rights
c. The United Nations Universal Declaration of Human Rights
d. None of these

65. Which of these is true about the U.S. Declaration of Independence?

a. It establishes political independence as a natural right
b. The "right of revolution" is not addressed in this text
c. Charges against King George III are in separate texts
d. It lacks John Locke's influence, found in British texts

66. Which of the following is accurate regarding the U.S. Constitutional Convention?

a. Those who were opposed to the Constitution's ratification were Federalists
b. All 13 states never had representation through the entire Convention
c. Thomas Jefferson, who influenced constitutional government, was present
d. Benjamin Franklin was popularly known as the "Father of the Constitution"

67. What is true regarding the League of Nations and its outcomes?

a. President Woodrow Wilson was always opposed to the U.S.'s membership
b. During its existence, the League of Nations never had any successes
c. It was limited by internal weaknesses and the U.S.'s failure to participate
d. It was reorganized after World War II to become the United Nations

68. Of the following, which statement is correct concerning the United Nations?

a. The United Nations does not incorporate a judicial department
b. The U.N.'s only important goal is to prevent international wars
c. The United Nations does not get involved with international law
d. The U.N. is involved in promoting world economic development

69. How is Mary Wollstonecraft Shelley's novel Frankenstein best described?

a. A Victorian expression of the repressed sexuality of the times
b. A poetic reflection on the "Satanic" nature of mechanization
c. A Romantic warning of the dual nature of scientific progress
d. A pure exercise in fantasy not reflecting any social concerns

70. What is the best characterization of Adam Smith's The Wealth of Nations in terms of its impact on economics?

a. Its impact was greater than that of Lavoisier's Traité Élémentaire de Chimie
b. Its impact was analogous to the impacts of Lavoisier's, Darwin's, and Newton's work in their respective fields
c. Its impact was lesser than that of Darwin's On the Origin of Species in biology
d. Its impact exceeded that of Newton's Principia Mathematica upon physics

71. Of the following scientists, who discovered the law defining the inverse relationship between the absolute pressure and volume of a gas?

a. Robert Boyle
b. Sir Francis Bacon
c. Sir Isaac Newton
d. Antoine Lavoisier

72. Who is considered the "Father of Geodesy (Geodetics)" and founder of mathematical geography?

a. Aristotle
b. Democritus
c. Archimedes
d. Eratosthenes

Answers and Explanations

1. A: Among his 95 Theses, which set off the Protestant Reformation, Martin Luther placed major emphasis on his opposition to the Catholic Church's practice of selling indulgences (cancellations of temporal punishment for forgiven sins). He cited simony—that is, buying and selling clerical positions—as well as the sale of indulgences as evidence of the Church's systemic corruption. Another Catholic practice Luther disagreed with was the celibacy of clerics, including monasticism. In addition, Luther and other Protestant reformers objected to most of the Catholic Church's seven sacraments.

2. B: The emphasis of the Protestant Reformers on the virtues of hard work has been credited with contributing to the development of modern capitalism and its success in improving the economies of those practicing it. The Protestant Reformation (Martin Luther posted his 95 Theses in 1517) triggered a series of many religious wars between opposing camps, which came to a head in the Thirty Years' War (1618–1648). The Treaty of Westphalia (1648) not only ended this war; it also eliminated the Pope's political authority and gave states the right to choose their religious denominations, thereby facilitating the further development of Protestantism.

3. C: More than half of all purchases of African slaves by European colonists were made in the 1700s by the British, Dutch, French, and Portuguese to labor in their colonies in Brazil and the Caribbean islands. Slightly more than 3% of the Atlantic slave trade took place in the 1500s. Roughly 16% of the Atlantic slave trade occurred during the 1600s. The boom in Atlantic slave trading of over 50% in the 1700s subsided in the 1800s to equal 28.5% of the total.

4. D: Increases in population growth supplied additional labor forces, helping to enable the Industrial Revolution. These increases were due to the prosperity brought through Europe's Commercial Revolution, which preceded the Industrial Revolution. The rediscovery of concrete, new advances in iron making, and the invention of the steam engine are all examples of developments that occurred during the Industrial Revolution.

5. B: The Industrial Revolution began in England when a series of inventions enabled the mechanization of industry that formerly depended on human manual and animal labor. From there, it spread to continental Europe, including France and Germany; thereafter, it reached North America and eventually spread throughout the entire world.

6. A: The Industrial Revolution did create a new working class composed of professionals like doctors and lawyers, industrialists, and businessmen. Formerly, Europe was dominated by royalty and landed gentry over the poor working class. Industrialization allowed many ordinary people to start and run businesses. It did NOT, however, improve working conditions in the 18th and early 19th centuries, but the opposite occurred: Big factories with machines made conditions more dangerous, and child labor caused many deaths, injuries, illnesses, and so on. Women and children were only banned from working in mines in the mid-19th century; housing and work conditions only improved in the late 19th century. Urbanization was the result of industrialization and not vice versa: Mechanization allowed factory construction, and people moved to cities for jobs. Labor unions developed out of the Industrial Revolution, not vice versa, to establish and defend factory workers' rights.

7. B: The Enlightenment strongly affected the thinking of Thomas Jefferson and Benjamin Franklin, thus directly influencing the American Revolution, America's Declaration of Independence, and the Constitution of the United States of America. The Enlightenment was an intellectual, political, cultural, and social movement, also known as the Age of Reason, which emphasized rational thought over religious dogma and not vice versa. Just as it influenced the American Revolution and Constitution, the Enlightenment also influenced the French Revolution and Constitution and not vice versa. In addition to those of America and France, Enlightenment ideals also informed the Polish–Lithuanian Constitution.

8. C: Standards of living went down for the majorities of Europe's and America's populations in the 18th century and most of the 19th century due to the Industrial Revolution because the majorities at that time were underpaid factory workers. Population growth, however, went up: For example, the population of Europe quadrupled between 1700 and 1900 with improvement in living conditions and health care. Public literacy also went up because the printing industry, like the textile industry before it, was afforded mass production through steam energy, expanding the publication of books and newspapers. Workers' earnings also went up: Though standards of living for industrial workers went down, their overall wages did ultimately increase from the early 19th century to the early 20th century as the changes of the Industrial Revolution led to worker unionization and new labor laws.

9. D: Scottish social philosopher and economist Adam Smith, author of The Wealth of Nations, disagreed with the mercantilist theory that wealth was automatically limited, was in favor of laissez-faire economics—that is, the government not interfering with commerce—and championed free trade. British political economist David Ricardo was also an advocate of free trade, and Scottish philosopher, historian, and economist David Hume also disagreed with the mercantilist theory of wealth. Smith is associated with both positions.

10. B: European colonization on other continents began in the 1400s and saw an exponential increase during the 1800s as innovations of the Industrial Revolution improved sea travel and international competition stimulated colonization. Spanish, Portuguese, Dutch, British, French, German, Italian, and Belgian visitors settled and conquered areas of Latin America, Asia, and Africa during these time periods.

11. C: Of the philosophers subscribing to the theory of the social contract as an agreement between people and their governments, Thomas Hobbes, author of Leviathan (1651), advocated absolute monarchy as the preferred social contract. Jean-Jacques Rousseau, author of The Social Contract (Du Contrat Social, 1762), advocated collective sovereignty and the general will of the people. Pierre-Joseph Proudhon (The General Idea of the Revolution in the 19th Century, 1851) advocated an individualist social contract based on individual sovereignty among individuals rather than between the individual or group and the state. John Locke, author of the Second Treatise of Government (1869), advocated social contracts based on natural human rights.

12. A: England did the most colonizing abroad during this period. However, it was not the first; the earliest European colonists were Dutch, Spanish, and Portuguese. These earliest colonizers were also the ones to keep some of their colonies the longest, into the 19th century. England did not dominate colonies in Southeast Asia and North Africa; these were areas colonized mainly by France, which was the runner-up to England in the areas it colonized.

13. D: In the last third of the 19th century, European imperialists had expanded to occupy territories on other continents. With the exception of the Dutch, Europeans colonized in Africa later than other continents because of the difficulties of distance, navigation, size, weather conditions, diseases, and so on. However, once other European colonizers reached Africa, they competed heavily over Africa. By the late 19th century, this competition included England, France, Germany, Italy, and Belgium.

14. A: By the end of the 1800s, the only countries fully independent of European imperialism were Ethiopia and Liberia, so not every African country was a European colony. The Sudan was briefly independent under Islamic Mahdi rule from 1885 to 1899 but was recaptured by Britain by 1899. What is Mali today was then the French Sudan, a colony of France. What is Malawi today was then Nyasaland, a British colony, as was Nigeria as well.

15. B: France was the location where historians consider the Enlightenment to have first begun. Influenced by French philosophers like Voltaire, Montesquieu, Bayle, and Rousseau (who was born and raised in Geneva, Switzerland, but spent time in Italy and France in his teens, moved to Paris by age 30, and died in France), intellectuals discussed new ideals in France's salons; Denis Diderot's Encyclopédie compiled contributions from hundreds of such thinkers, allowing their ideas to be transmitted further. From France, the cultural movement of the Enlightenment spread to Britain and the rest of the United Kingdom and thereafter to Germany, Holland, Russia, Italy, and Spain. Once Europe had embraced the Enlightenment, it then spread to Europe's American colonies, influencing the architects of American independence.

16. C: The Ottoman Empire joined with the Central Powers in 1914 during World War I. The original Triple Alliance was formed by Austria-Hungary, Germany, and Italy in 1882 and renewed in 1902. The Ottoman Empire signed the Turco-German Alliance in August 1914, joining with the Central Powers. In October 1914, with the bombing of Russian ports on the Black Sea, Turkey formally entered World War I. The Allied Powers of the Triple Entente (Great Britain, France, and Russia) declared war on the Ottoman Empire in November 1914.

17. D: A Serbian nationalist group called the Black Hand felt that Bosnia should belong to Serbia, which was ruled by Austria-Hungary then. They assassinated the heir to Austria-Hungary's throne, Archduke Franz Ferdinand of Austria, and his wife. Austria reacted by declaring war on Serbia. Then, Germany pledged its support to Austria-Hungary, whereupon Russia pledged its support to Serbia. Germany reacted to Russia's pledge by declaring war on Russia. France pledged to support Russia and Germany then declared war on France, and so on, in a domino effect.

18. A: Hitler had agreed to a nonaggression pact in 1934. He violated the terms of this pact in 1939 by invading Poland with the intent of acquiring it for Germany. Germany was issued an ultimatum by Britain and France, not America. They demanded that he withdraw from Poland, or they would declare war. Hitler refused to withdraw, and World War II started. The Soviet Union did invade Poland, but after Germany did, not before, and after the war began. Two years after Germany attacked Poland, Hitler also invaded the Soviet Union in 1941 and not vice versa.

19. C: It is correct that, after World War II ended, the United States formed the North Atlantic Treaty Organization (NATO) among European and North American countries to be a defensive military alliance. The North Atlantic Treaty was signed in 1949. The adversarial relationship between the USSR and USA began during the Cold War due to conflicts between Democratic and Communist ideologies; it was not a continuation of World War II conditions as Russia and America were allies against Nazi Germany during that war. The Marshall Plan was implemented not to contain Communism but to help postwar Europe recover and rebuild. The Truman Doctrine was designed not to help rebuild Europe, but to contain the spread of Communism by pledging to defend any countries threatened by being involuntarily overtaken by Communists.

20. B: Fascism did spread in Italy, Spain, and Germany, but prior to World War II. Post-World War I angst, as well as the depression of the 1930s, fostered the rise of Fascism, which came to a head in the Second World War. The Cold War followed World War II, lasting from the mid-1940s until 1991, and included the nuclear arms race (A). Although the United States ended World War II by bombing

Hiroshima and Nagasaki in Japan, these two countries later became allies (C). The recent modernization and industrialization of Japan gave it a strong economy, which helped motivate both nations to become allies rather than enemies. Most of the European powers' colonies were decolonized after World War II and gained freedom (D).

21. D: The Hudson River, its tributaries, and many additional creeks in the area provided abundant water supplies for European immigrants settling in the New York City area. Geographically, this site also had the Appalachian and Catskill Mountain ranges to provide the advantages of natural protective barriers. This area also had many trees, providing building materials for settlers as well as other natural resources. New York City is a site geographically located on the coast. This afforded a natural harbor, allowing new arrivals to settle without additional, overland travel; to fish for food; and to start fishing businesses. Having a seaport also enabled easier travel to and from the site for trade.

22. C: The Panama Canal, though only half the length of the Suez Canal, was harder to build due to geographic barriers, especially the continental divide's high altitude, which necessitated building locks to connect segments of varying heights. Tropical diseases also impeded work, as did political corruption in the French government causing money shortages. French project leader Ferdinand de Lesseps abandoned the Panama Canal in 1889. Americans undertook its completion when the Spanish–American War made them realize its military advantages. They completed it in 1914, but a landslide delayed its official opening until 1920. The Suez had fewer natural obstacles and the advantage of five natural lakes. De Lesseps also led the Suez Canal Company and completed that project by 1869.

23. B: Queen Elizabeth I established an English Protestant church that would eventually develop into the Church of England. She governed less strictly and more moderately than her father, Henry VIII; her brother, Edward VI; or her sister, Mary I. England's Royal Navy defeated the Spanish Armada in 1588, during Elizabeth's reign from 1558 to 1603, and she became associated with this famed military victory. Elizabeth did have many courtships in her life, but she was never actually married and thus became known as the Virgin Queen.

24. C: Queen Victoria reigned over England and the United Kingdom for an astonishing 63 years and 7 months, longer than any other female monarch in history and longer than any other British monarch. England (and the United Kingdom) had become a constitutional monarchy before she became queen. While this gave the monarch little political power, Victoria worked privately to influence government appointments and policy, while publicly, she attained the status of a national icon associated with strict moral standards. During her long reign, the British Empire expanded greatly. Victoria did inherit the throne at the age of 18; however, she was married to Prince Albert, her first cousin, from 1840 until his death in 1861. They had nine children and 34 grandchildren, 26 of whom lived to adulthood.

25. C: One of the provisions of the English Bill of Rights was to restore the rights of Protestants to bear arms after King James II had deprived them of this right. It also stipulated no royal interference with the rights of all citizens to arm themselves as permitted by law. The English Bill of Rights was not first ratified in the 18th century but the 17th, in 1689. It did not make Church courts legal; it dictated that only civil courts were legal and not Church courts. The English Bill of Rights also prohibits royalty from levying any new taxes, from acting as judges, and from creating new courts without consent of Parliament. Generally, the English Bill of Rights limits the powers of monarchy and requires most governmental actions to be jointly decided by Parliament and monarchs.

26. D: The U.S. Bill of Rights was adopted by the House of Representatives August 21, 1789. It was formally proposed by a joint resolution of the U.S. Congress September 25, 1789. It was ratified by three quarters of the states, becoming effective December 15, 1791. It is not a separate document from Constitutional amendments: The U.S. Bill of Rights consists of the first ten amendments to the U.S. Constitution. The purpose of the Bill of Rights was to limit federal government's power, not increase it. It was not written and offered to Congress by Thomas Jefferson, the primary author of the Declaration of Independence; it was written and presented to Congress by James Madison, then a congressman from Virginia in the House of Representatives and later the fourth president of the U.S. from 1801 to 1809.

27. D: The French Declaration of the Rights of Man and of the Citizen (Déclaration des droits de l'Homme et du Citoyen, 1789) omitted any mention of the matter of slavery and also did not address the rights of women, who were not considered citizens at the time. Accordingly, in 1791, the Declaration of the Rights of Woman and the Female Citizen, based closely on the 1789 Declaration but specifying female rights, was published by women's rights advocates. The last of the 17 articles of the Declaration of the Rights of Man and of the Citizen states the "inviolable and sacred right" to property.

28. A: The original reason the Federal Convention convened in 1787 was to revise the existing Articles of Confederation of the United States. However, members soon realized that this would not accomplish their aims, and they would need instead to draft an entirely new document. This new document became the U.S. Constitution. One issue important to members of the Convention was how much power should be given to the central federal government. Another important issue was how many representatives each state should have in Congress. Some thought it should be uniform, while others argued it should vary according to the size of each state's population. An additional issue also discussed at this Convention was whether representatives in Congress should be elected directly by the people or by state legislatures.

29. B: President Woodrow Wilson strongly advocated that the U.S. join the League of Nations. The last of his Fourteen Points stated that such a group should be formed. The League of Nations was the very first international peacekeeping organization; it did not follow a series of such groups. Despite Wilson's advocacy and the many other world nations that joined, America never actually joined the League of Nations or ratified its covenant. This was due to opposition by the Republican Party and also to Wilson's refusing to compromise on its terms. The League of Nations ultimately failed in its mission to prevent war: It was formed in 1919 after World War I and had its first meeting in 1920, and World War II erupted in 1939.

30. D: The Protestant work ethic is considered by many historians to have contributed to the Industrial Revolution. In Britain, where industrialization started, financial stability encouraged investment in industry, and the eventual dominance of Protestantism is believed to have contributed to a class of entrepreneurs who believed in education, technological progress, and hard work. The other choices are considered effects of industrialization. Mass production enabled the privately owned, for-profit enterprises that characterize capitalist economic systems. Socialism developed as a criticism of capitalism; Karl Marx argued that capitalism polarized societies into owners versus workers. Marx also viewed capitalism as a necessary precursor to socialism within the logical progression of economies. Romanticism also developed in reaction against mechanization, contrasting nature as more valuable in art and language versus the dark side of scientific progress.

31. A: The first edition of Smith's masterpiece was published in 1776. In England's 1777 budget, Prime Minister Lord North, inspired by Smith's book, proposed two new taxes on auctioned property and manservants. The 1778 budget introduced the malt tax and inhabited house duty, both advocated by Smith. Opinions of Smith and his book varied among English radicals. For example, radical Thomas Paine (Common Sense) wrote The Rights of Man in 1791, criticizing that, if only Edmund Burke had "talents similar" to those of Smith, he might understand the components of a constitution. On the other hand, in 1826, English radical William Cobbett attacked Smith, the Edinburgh Review, the Scottish political economy, the Poor Law, and political economists in general. Smith's book was quoted by those opposing war: In the London Times in 1803, an article argued that continuing peaceful commercial trade with Spain was more profitable than any war. William Wilberforce quoted The Wealth of Nations when introducing his bill against the slave trade.

32. B: Marie Sklodovska Curie won the Nobel Prize for Physics, shared with husband Pierre Curie and fellow researcher Henri Becquerel, in 1903. In 1911, she won the Nobel Prize for Chemistry. Mme. Curie—who discovered, named, and formulated a theory of radioactivity; discovered two new radioactive elements; developed methods to isolate radioactive isotopes; and pioneered radiation therapy—was the first and one of two people to win two Nobel Prizes in different fields and the only person ever to win for multiple sciences. Linus Pauling won Nobel Prizes for Chemistry in 1954 and Peace in 1962. Albert Einstein won many awards, including the 1921 Nobel Prize for Physics. Thomas Alva Edison invented the electric light bulb, phonograph, motion picture camera, and many others and is credited with creating the first industrial research laboratory. Edison received many awards. In 1915, the New York Times reported Edison was to share a Nobel Prize with Nicola Tesla, but this did not happen. Reasons for this report and its contradiction are unknown.

33. D: French chemist Louis Pasteur (1822–1895), considered one of the founders of bacteriology, developed a process of heating and cooling food products like milk and wine that reduces the number of pathogenic microbes to a level that will not cause sickness when ingested. This process is named pasteurization after him. Pasteur also made the first vaccines against both rabies and anthrax. All three of these accomplishments were incredible breakthroughs in preventing fatal diseases. Pasteur's experiments advanced the germ theory of disease, which when first proposed, met strong resistance from those who did not believe microorganisms cause sickness. His work supported its acceptance and colleague Robert Koch's proof of it in 1890.

34. C: The Jesuits, a Catholic religious order, mounted the Counterreformation in reaction to the Protestant Reformation led by Martin Luther, John Calvin, and others. The Counterreformation restored Poland and other large parts of Europe to Catholicism. The Anglicans were one of the largest new Protestant denominations and were based in England. The Lutherans, named after Martin Luther, were another large, new Protestant denomination living in Germany and Scandinavia. The Reformed Churches were also one of the largest new Protestant denominations found in Scotland, the Netherlands, Switzerland, and Germany. The Protestant Reformation also included many other, smaller Protestant denominations.

35. B: Among a great many differences of opinion the Protestant Reformers found against the Catholic Church, one was its beliefs about the intercession of the saints and its devotion to them. They opposed many Catholic doctrines, including the Pope's authority, the usage and sale of indulgences, and the doctrine of transubstantiation. Moreover, they disagreed with Catholic attitudes toward Mary, particularly in seeing the Catholic veneration of Mary as idolatrous worship.

36. C: While various issues Martin Luther raised in his 95 Theses have often been cited as central, including the Catholic selling of indulgences, belief in purgatory, belief in the Pope's infallibility, and the issue of the Pope's political authority, Luther himself wrote that these were trivial compared to the truly central issue: the Catholic doctrine of free will. In 1524, Desiderius Erasmus had published

De Libero Arbitrio (On Free Will), attacking Luther's beliefs. In 1525, Luther replied, refuting Erasmus in his De Servo Arbitrio (On the Bondage of the Will, or literally, On the Unfree Will). He wrote that "the papacy, purgatory, indulgences and such like . . ." were "trifles, rather than issues . . ." and thanked Erasmus for attacking "the real thing, that is, the essential issue," that is, free will. Luther believed that, after Adam's fall, free will had no meaning.

37. D: The ancient Mayan civilization was located in what are today Guatemala, Belize, Honduras, and El Salvador in Central America and also in the Yucatan peninsula and the south of Mexico. The ancient civilization of the Incas was located in what is now Peru in South America. The ancient civilization of the Aztecs lived in what is Mexico today.

38. A: There are many descendants of the ancient Mayans still living today in southern Mexico, Central America, and on the Yucatan peninsula. However, the Aztec and Inca civilizations were destroyed in the 16th century by the Spanish conquistadores, who first exposed them to foreign diseases like smallpox, decimating the natives' numbers, and then attacked and killed the remaining populations. The Mayans' decentralization allowed them to resist these invaders for 170 years, and moreover, many independent states enabled their peoples to survive even after Spanish political conquest.

39. B: The Aztec civilization was destroyed by the Spanish by 1521, after conquistadores, in 1520, mainly led by Cortés, killed Aztec Emperor Montezuma, who had ruled for 17 years, which was followed by subsequent smallpox epidemics and Spanish destruction of the Aztec capital city of Tenochtitlan. The Incan civilization was also invaded by the Spanish, especially Pizarro. Conquistadores captured the Incas' last stronghold in 1572. Thereafter, they eradicated much of Incan culture, including the methodical destruction of their advanced farming system. The Incas' advanced road system likely contributed to the spread of smallpox from South America and other foreign diseases, delivering the final blow. The Mayans had no capital or political center to destroy; their independent states, scattered over more areas, resisted conquest for 170 years after Spanish arrivals, which never wiped out their population.

40. C: Before the Atlantic slave trade began in the 15th century, slavery was already a common practice in Asia, Africa, Europe, and the Americas. In Africa, those engaged in internal wars would enslave those they captured. Africa also had commercial slave dealers; Europe and America became additional markets for their existing businesses of selling slaves. Buying and using slaves were also common practices in Asia, Europe, and the Americas, even before the Atlantic systems of slave trading.

41. D: James Watt, a Scottish engineer, invented the modern version of the steam engine in 1769 and made further improvements to it in 1784. This was a hallmark of the Industrial Revolution because manufacturing no longer depended on being located near a river or stream for water power. Without this site restriction, factories were then built in much greater numbers, leading to mechanized mass production. Portuguese explorer Vasco da Gama sailed around the Cape of Good Hope, Africa, in 1497. This gave European traders a new commercial route not already dominated by Italian city-states and Ottoman Turks, shifting Europe's commercial center from the Mediterranean to Western Europe. Competition among nations also accelerated the drive to colonize. And, the practice of new financial activities like banking, stock investments, and insurance began. These developments all occurred during Europe's Commercial Revolution, bringing prosperity and allowing population growth, which provided enough labor forces to enable the Industrial Revolution that followed.

42. A: The textile industry was revolutionized in England through the inventions of the flying shuttle, the water frame, the spinning jenny, and the spinning mule, which all enabled much faster spinning of yarn to make fabric. This led to many new cotton mills being built. Cottage industries, that is, small-scale, home-based work by artisans, were replaced in the Industrial Revolution by the factory system. There was no concrete industry until 1756, when English engineer John Smeaton rediscovered this compound, which had been forgotten since the 5th century. Making concrete also supported the construction of mills and factories. Water mills were the only kinds of mills possible before the Industrial Revolution. James Watt's invention of the modern steam engine allowed mills and factories to be built in many more places instead of just near running streams of water.

43. B: In England, the Trade Union Act was passed in 1871, allowing trade unions* to be registered by the Registrar of Friendly Societies, making their activities legal and protecting their monies. The earliest event of these choices was the first Factory Act passed in 1819, which made it unlawful for children under the age of 9 to work in factories and limited the work hours of children, aged 9 to 16 to 72 hours weekly. The Combination Acts of 1799 and 1800, which had made trade unions illegal, were repealed in 1824. Despite a new Combination Act in 1825 limiting union activities, trade unions continued to form. The Ten Hours Act, restricting the work hours of women and youth to 10 hours a day, passed in 1847. *Note: The term trade union in England is labor union in America.

44. D: Enlightenment thinkers stressed the important roles of rational thinking and knowledge in reforming society. They supported the spirit and practice of intellectual inquiry and discourse while denouncing corruption, abuse, and intolerance in religious and political institutions. In the Enlightenment, the perception was that public opinion took precedence over the positions of leaders, which had been more powerful in pre-Enlightenment and pre-Revolutionary monarchies. The Enlightenment also found the methods of empirical science more objective, provable, and hence defensible than beliefs in religious dogma. Enlightenment ideals did not differ drastically from modern Western beliefs; they were actually the basis for today's Western political and intellectual culture.

45. C: Inventions and improvements of the Industrial Revolution transformed many businesses from small-scale operations using manual labor to large-scale factory operations using machines. Included in these was the publishing industry. With the application of steam power, books, newspapers, and magazines could be printed in far greater numbers with far greater speed. This increased access to reading materials promoted public literacy. The more the public read, the more knowledge they gained, and the more they demanded to participate in politics. Factory workers as a group did not ignore politics due to work schedules. The Luddites did form as a reaction against industrialization. They did not aid public political action; they protested technological progress in general and sometimes sabotaged factory machines. Industrialization did foster greater interest in capitalism but not at the expense of politics.

46. D: According to some economists, a key difference between the earlier mercantilism and the later capitalism brought through the Industrial Revolution was that, whereas products were commodities in mercantilism, the production factors of land, labor, and money also became commodities in capitalism. Once these elements needed to process or manufacture goods became treated and regarded as saleable goods in themselves, labor markets accordingly became generalized rather than specialized.

47. A: Spanish conquistadores were the earliest to visit and conquer the Latin American countries in the 15th century. Europeans then also occupied seaports in Asia and Africa. Except for the Dutch in the 17th century, continental Africa was not colonized by most other Europeans until the 19th century because of the challenges presented against travel and settlement by geography, climate, and diseases.

48. B: Denis Diderot was a French philosopher, art critic, and author. He wrote novels, plays, essays, and many articles on Enlightenment philosophy as others did; however, he was most famed as cofounder, editor, and contributor to the Encyclopédie, which was highly instrumental in disseminating the ideas of the Enlightenment. John Locke was known as the "Father of Liberalism;" Baruch Spinoza was known as one of the preeminent Rationalist philosophers of the 17th century; and Sir Isaac Newton established new laws of physics and mathematical concepts. These philosophers were among those who inspired the Enlightenment. Diderot is best known for helping this movement to spread throughout the world by publishing his encyclopedia.

49. D: John Locke's idea of the social contract was the one adopted by the authors of the United States Declaration of Independence. His concept was of a contract between people and state based on natural human rights that could not be denied. Rousseau's idea of the social contract was based on popular sovereignty, that is, government by the people; he did not believe in representative government. Thomas Hobbes's idea of the social contract was of one between the people and an absolute ruler. He believed that the natural state only produced anarchy; that individual self-interest was superseded by the rights and contracts that form society and, hence, the states' need to protect those rights; and that states' self-interests would conflict, necessitating a leader's sovereignty over states to impose social contract laws. Philosopher David Hume is less associated with social contract theory. He believed that government should be based on contract but also that contract was an artifice. He shared empiricism with Locke and compatibilism of free will and determinism with Hobbes.

50. C: The earliest European colonizers of other continents came from Holland, Spain, and Portugal. These countries also retained some of their colonies as late as the 19th century. Germany and Italy did not begin to colonize around the same time as England and France; because both countries were divided internally and each was not unified until the 1860s, they were later to begin colonization. England and France were the biggest colonizers of countries overseas but did not keep some colonies as long as Holland, Spain, and Portugal did. The Dutch Boers first settled in Africa in the 1600s, while the Spaniards began conquering Latin American countries in the 1500s.

51. C: England was the official owner of the Nile River, which was likely Africa's most valuable asset as a natural navigation route. England had colonized Egypt and a great number of other African countries by the late 19th century. The Nile, the world's longest river, runs through 11 African countries, many of which were British colonies at the time. Belgium occupied the Congo then but not the Nile.

52. D: The French government was very hostile to the ideas of the Enlightenment, such that these ideas were ultimately expressed violently in the French Revolution's overthrowing the monarchy. German government was not threatened by the movement, which strongly influenced its middle-class spiritually and nationalistically. The Enlightenment was not a reaction against Romanticism; the Romantic Movement took place after the Enlightenment as a reaction against its rationalism. There was indeed such a thing as a Counter-Enlightenment; it was antirational and strongly associated with German Romanticism. Some European rulers did accept and even embrace Enlightenment ideas; called "enlightened despots" by historians, they included Prussia's Frederick the Great, Russia's Empress Catherine the Great, and Austria's Emperor Joseph II, as well as Portugal's Senior Minister Pombal and Denmark's Senior Minister Struensee.

53. A: Italy had formed the Triple Alliance with Germany and Austria-Hungary in the late 1800s. This alliance lasted until 1914. However, Germany's and Austria-Hungary's actions in going to war were offensive, whereas the Triple Alliance was a defensive military agreement, so Italy refused to participate and subsequently switched its allegiance to the Triple Entente of Britain, France, and Russia to enter the conflict in 1915 against Austria-Hungary and against Germany in 1916.

54. B: The first nation Germany declared war against was Russia at the start of World War I. The first actual declaration of war was by Austria, not Germany, against Serbia after a Serbian nationalist group assassinated Austrian Archduke Franz Ferdinand and his wife. When Austria declared war, Germany pledged support to Austria, and Russia pledged support to Serbia. Germany then declared war against Russia for supporting Serbia. When France pledged its support to Russia, Germany also declared war on France. On its way to invade France, Germany also invaded Belgium. England then pledged to support Belgium and declared war on Germany.

55. C: For the first two years of World War II, America adhered to policies of neutrality and isolationism, as it had also done for the first three years of World War I. The Japanese did not formally declare war on America but staged a surprise attack on Pearl Harbor in 1941 as well as another attack on Allied colonies in Thailand, Malaya, and Hong Kong with the intent of taking Allied colonies and conquering Southeast Asia. The USA responded to this surprise attack by declaring war on Japan and entering WWII. Britain and other Allies also declared war on Japan. The Axis powers responded by declaring war on the Allies. In fact, when America declared war on Germany and Italy, Germany and Italy declared war on America on the same day. America demanded Japan's unconditional surrender first, bombing Hiroshima and Nagasaki after Japan refused. This first and only use of atomic bombs in 1945 caused Japan to surrender.

56. D: All of these events took place during the Cold War period, which was from 1945 to 1991. The Berlin Airlift, wherein America and Britain flew supplies into Berlin after the Soviets blockaded the city, took place from 1948 to 1949. The Korean War took place from 1950 to 1953, with American forces defending South Korea against communist North Korea with support from the United Nations. The war in Vietnam lasted from 1959 to 1975 between communist North Vietnam and its allies and South Vietnam, which America and other anticommunist countries supported. Additional Cold War conflicts involving the USA against the Soviets included the Berlin Crisis in 1961 and the 1962 Cuban Missile Crisis, both during John F. Kennedy's presidency, and the Soviet war in Afghanistan from 1979 to 1989.

57. B: England did not keep its isolationist policy toward continental Europe in the late 19th to early 20th centuries. England had held this policy for almost 100 years but ended its isolationism by forming the Entente Cordiale with France in 1904. France made the separation of church and state official (A) in 1900. While England maintained its enormous British Empire during this period, it did fall behind Germany and the United States in industrial production rates (C). During the 19th century, the Slavic Orthodox peoples in Eastern Europe revolted several times against the declining Ottoman Empire, creating Slavic Orthodox nations. Russia supported these nations in a policy known as Pan-Slavism. This policy caused conflicts between the Ottoman Empire and the Austro-Hungarian Empire (D).

58. A: Rivers promoted the development of the ancient river valley civilizations of the world, including in the Middle East, India, and China. Rivers not only supply water for drinking and crop irrigation, but also provide fertile soil, vegetation for shade cover, food, building materials, and animal life. They additionally allow water travel to other locations. Although some peoples have settled and lived in deserts, they are among the most inhospitable climates. Forests also provide plenty of flora and fauna and exist in areas receiving enough rainfall, but rivers have been historically superior in attracting human societies. Mountains near living areas provide protective barriers; however, though some peoples live there, as in deserts, living in the mountains is difficult due to high altitudes, harsh climates, poor soil for planting, and rough terrain.

59. C: The Suez and Panama Canals share in common political controversy that developed over control of each of these strategic waterways. The French started the Suez Canal Company in 1858 with Egyptian support and began digging in 1859. However, England bought a large share of the Suez Canal Company in 1875; Egypt seized the canal in 1956, starting much debate and a short war. Though less violent, long-term discussions and tensions between America and Panama surrounded the Panama Canal, leading to two 1977 treaties agreeing to Panama's controlling the canal while maintaining some U.S. rights related to it. Both the Suez and Panama are among the world's most important, and largest, canals. Both took much manual labor, but the Panama was much harder to build than the Suez due to tropical diseases, rougher terrain, and high altitudes requiring digging trenches, damming a river, and building canal locks. The Suez had far fewer natural barriers and five natural lakes. Therefore, the two were not constructed under similar geographical conditions.

60. D: Judaism has existed since around 1300 B.C. according to historians' estimates. The Greek religion of Stoicism was founded by Zeno in Athens around 313 B.C., almost 1,000 years later than Judaism. Confucianism was founded in China by Confucius, who lived from 551 to 479 B.C., around 800 years after Judaism. Christianity dates to approximately 30 A.D. in Israel.

61. D: Christianity is practiced by the most people in the world, with an estimated 2 billion followers (all denominations combined). Islam is second (all denominations including Sunni and Shi'ite), with about 1.3 billion adherents. Hinduism is practiced by some 900 million people. Buddhism (all sects and schools) has at least 360 million followers in the world.

62. C: During Elizabeth I's reign over England and Ireland, known as the Elizabethan era, playwrights such as William Shakespeare, Christopher Marlowe, Ben Jonson, and a great many others produced dramatic masterpieces of the English Renaissance. The Elizabethan era was also known for nautical exploration by Sir Francis Drake and others. Elizabeth's foreign policies were very conservative and cautious in general. Under her rule, England's famous defeat of the Spanish Armada in 1588 was only achieved after Spain's invasion with the intent to conquer Britain gave it no choice but to retaliate, resulting in England's most famous military victory. Elizabeth's 44-year reign provided her subjects with greater stability and a stronger sense of national identity after the shorter reigns of her half-sister Mary I and her half-brother Edward VI.

63. B: Queen Victoria's prime ministers' 20 terms were divided equally between Conservatives (formerly Tories) and Liberals (formerly Whigs). Including multiple (nonconsecutive) terms by Lord Derby, Lord Russell, Lord Palmerston, Benjamin Disraeli, William Gladstone, and Lord Salisbury, her reign had 10 terms of Conservatives and 10 of Liberals. Victoria was the victim of more than one assassination attempt: two in 1842, one in 1849, one in 1850, and one in 1882. Despite being called the "Famine Queen" in Ireland and a popular myth that she only donated £5 to Ireland during its Great Potato Famine, Victoria actually made a personal donation of £2,000, more than any other single donor, for Irish famine relief. She also supported a grant to a Roman Catholic seminary in Ireland over Protestant objections. Victoria worked to better English–French relations. She and Albert exchanged visits with King Louis Philippe—being the first British rulers to visit a French ruler in over 300 years and Louis Philippe the first French king to visit British monarchs—and with Napoleon III.

64. D: The English Bill of Rights is known to have influenced the United States of America's Bill of Rights, the European Convention on Human Rights, and the United National Universal Declaration of Human Rights, as well as the Canadian Charter of Rights and Freedoms. All of these documents contain many similar provisions, such as those regarding the rights to life, liberty, and security; freedom of speech; freedom of assembly; the right to bear arms; those prohibiting cruel and unusual punishment and arbitrary detention or imprisonment, and so on.

65. A: The United States Declaration of Independence states in its very first sentence that "one people" is entitled "to assume among the powers of the earth, the separate and equal station" by "the laws of Nature and of Nature's God . . ." In other words, this is a natural right. The Declaration also addresses the "right of revolution" in its preamble; that is, people have the right to change or get rid of any government that violates the people's God-given "unalienable rights." The Declaration includes a long list of charges against King George III of England for violating such rights; these are not in a separate text. The U.S. Declaration of Independence shares the influence of political philosopher John Locke with the English Declaration and Bill of Rights, which influenced it. Locke's ideas were highly influential to the Enlightenment, the English Bill of Rights, the American Revolution, and the Declaration of Independence among others.

66. B: Throughout the meetings of the U.S. Constitutional Convention, there was never a time when all 13 states had representation. Two of New York's deputies left the Convention less than two months after it convened. Alexander Hamilton, the third deputy, did not cast New York's vote while in attendance. The deputies from New Hampshire only arrived two months after the meeting assembled with a quorum. Rhode Island never sent any deputies to the Convention. Hence the Convention votes never exceeded 11 states at any time. The Federalists advocated ratifying the Constitution; the Antifederalists opposed it. Thomas Jefferson did influence constitutional government; for example, he pushed for adoption of the Bill of Rights containing the first ten Amendments. However, he was not present at the Convention as he was America's Minister to France at the time. Benjamin Franklin was known as the "Sage of the Constitutional Convention." James Madison was known as the "Father of the Constitution."

67. C: There were internal weaknesses inside the organization of the League of Nations that limited its effectiveness. Another major factor limiting its powers was the fact that the United States never ratified the League of Nations Covenant and never joined the League. President Wilson was not opposed to U.S. membership; the fourteenth of his Fourteen Points called for such an organization to be founded, and he conducted a vigorous nationwide campaign for the U.S. to join the League. However, when compromises were proposed, Wilson would not accept them, and the United States' Republican Party was also against joining. The League did have several noteworthy successes during the 1920s. However, it ultimately failed in its mission of world disarmament and failed to prevent World War II only 21 years after the end of World War I, 20 years after the League's formation, and 19 years after the first League meeting. It was not reorganized into the UN; it was officially disbanded in 1946 and replaced by the United Nations, a different organization.

68. D: The United Nations has a number of goals, including promoting world economic development and international economic and social cooperation. The UN does include a judicial organ, its International Court of Justice. Preventing international wars is one of the UN's important goals but not the only one; it also aims to promote cooperation in international law, human rights, social progress, international security, and ultimately, its wish is to accomplish world peace.

69. C: Mary Wollstonecraft married the great Romantic poet Percy Bysshe Shelley. This couple, plus famous Romantic poet George Gordon, Lord Byron, and John Polidori, author of Vampyre, the first English-language vampire novel, agreed to a contest to see who could write the best horror story. This resulted in Mary Shelley's Frankenstein (1818, 1823). By depicting a scientist who experiments to create life and succeeds but is horrified by the outcome, Shelley dramatized the idea that scientific progress could backfire and produce not only benefits but also horrors. The Romantic Movement was in the late 18th and early to mid-19th centuries; Frankenstein predated the Victorian era (1837–1901) and is not viewed as an expression of repressed sexuality. A poetic reflection on the "satanic" nature of mechanization is found in the Romantic poetry of William Blake, particularly his description of "dark satanic mills" in his poem "And Did Those Feet in Ancient Time." While the story of Frankenstein was a fantasy, it was not unreflective of social concerns (see above).

70. B: Adam Smith's The Wealth of Nations (1776) created a fundamental shift in the entire philosophical view of economics that was analogous to the change wrought in the field of chemistry by Antoine Lavoisier's Traité Élémentaire de Chimie (Elementary Treatise on Chemistry, 1789), which introduced the first list of elements, the precursor to the modern periodic table of elements, and is regarded as the first modern chemistry text. The Wealth of Nations revolutionized economics similarly to the way Charles Darwin's On the Origin of Species (1859) revolutionized biology by introducing the theory of evolution. The impact of Smith's economic masterpiece can also be compared to the impact on the field of physics caused by Sir Isaac Newton's Principia Mathematica (Principles of Mathematics), wherein he introduced his Laws of Motion and other principles, illuminating natural processes not previously understood.

71. A: Robert Boyle (1627–1691) defined Boyle's Law, stating that, in a closed system and at a constant temperature, the absolute pressure of a gas and its volume are inversely proportional; that is, as one increases, the other decreases in equal amounts. Sir Francis Bacon (1561–1626) was a pioneer of the scientific method and is called the "Father of Empiricism." Although Boyle denied being influenced by or even studying Bacon or others, his asset as a researcher was that he adhered to Bacon's method. Sir Isaac Newton (1642–1727) was an alchemist like Boyle and was influenced by Boyle. He defined the three Laws of Motion and universal gravitation; formed theories and laws in optics, acoustics, thermodynamics, and calculus as well as physics; and is considered the founder of classical mechanics. Antoine Lavoisier (1743–1794) was one of the fathers of modern chemistry. He discovered and named the gases oxygen and hydrogen; made the first list of the elements; helped create the metric system; and defined the law that the mass of matter remains constant despite shape or form.

72. D: Eratosthenes (circa 276–195 B.C.), a Libyan mathematician, poet, athlete, astronomer, and music theorist who studied and worked in ancient Greece, was first to use the word geography and originated it as a discipline. He was first to calculate accurately both the circumference and the tilt of the Earth. He invented a system of latitude and longitude, created a world map, and also founded scientific chronology. The ancient Greek philosopher, scientist, and polymath Aristotle (circa 384–322 B.C.) made zoological observations confirmed accurate in the 19th century and has sometimes been called the "Father of Biology." Ancient Greek philosopher and scientist Democritus (circa 460–370 B.C.) is regarded as the "Father of Early Atomic Theory" for founding the cosmological philosophy of atomism. Archimedes (circa 287–212 B.C.), one of the great ancient Greek scientists and considered among the greatest mathematicians of all time, was friends with Eratosthenes. He founded statics and hydrostatics, defined the principle of levers, and invented many original machines.

How to Overcome Test Anxiety

Just the thought of taking a test is enough to make most people a little nervous. A test is an important event that can have a long-term impact on your future, so it's important to take it seriously and it's natural to feel anxious about performing well. But just because anxiety is normal, that doesn't mean that it's helpful in test taking, or that you should simply accept it as part of your life. Anxiety can have a variety of effects. These effects can be mild, like making you feel slightly nervous, or severe, like blocking your ability to focus or remember even a simple detail.

If you experience test anxiety—whether severe or mild—it's important to know how to beat it. To discover this, first you need to understand what causes test anxiety.

Causes of Test Anxiety

While we often think of anxiety as an uncontrollable emotional state, it can actually be caused by simple, practical things. One of the most common causes of test anxiety is that a person does not feel adequately prepared for their test. This feeling can be the result of many different issues such as poor study habits or lack of organization, but the most common culprit is time management. Starting to study too late, failing to organize your study time to cover all of the material, or being distracted while you study will mean that you're not well prepared for the test. This may lead to cramming the night before, which will cause you to be physically and mentally exhausted for the test. Poor time management also contributes to feelings of stress, fear, and hopelessness as you realize you are not well prepared but don't know what to do about it.

Other times, test anxiety is not related to your preparation for the test but comes from unresolved fear. This may be a past failure on a test, or poor performance on tests in general. It may come from comparing yourself to others who seem to be performing better or from the stress of living up to expectations. Anxiety may be driven by fears of the future—how failure on this test would affect your educational and career goals. These fears are often completely irrational, but they can still negatively impact your test performance.

Elements of Test Anxiety

As mentioned earlier, test anxiety is considered to be an emotional state, but it has physical and mental components as well. Sometimes you may not even realize that you are suffering from test anxiety until you notice the physical symptoms. These can include trembling hands, rapid heartbeat, sweating, nausea, and tense muscles. Extreme anxiety may lead to fainting or vomiting. Obviously, any of these symptoms can have a negative impact on testing. It is important to recognize them as soon as they begin to occur so that you can address the problem before it damages your performance.

The mental components of test anxiety include trouble focusing and inability to remember learned information. During a test, your mind is on high alert, which can help you recall information and stay focused for an extended period of time. However, anxiety interferes with your mind's natural processes, causing you to blank out, even on the questions you know well. The strain of testing during anxiety makes it difficult to stay focused, especially on a test that may take several hours. Extreme anxiety can take a huge mental toll, making it difficult not only to recall test information but even to understand the test questions or pull your thoughts together.

Effects of Test Anxiety

Test anxiety is like a disease—if left untreated, it will get progressively worse. Anxiety leads to poor performance, and this reinforces the feelings of fear and failure, which in turn lead to poor performances on subsequent tests. It can grow from a mild nervousness to a crippling condition. If allowed to progress, test anxiety can have a big impact on your schooling, and consequently on your future.

Test anxiety can spread to other parts of your life. Anxiety on tests can become anxiety in any stressful situation, and blanking on a test can turn into panicking in a job situation. But fortunately, you don't have to let anxiety rule your testing and determine your grades. There are a number of relatively simple steps you can take to move past anxiety and function normally on a test and in the rest of life.

Physical Steps for Beating Test Anxiety

While test anxiety is a serious problem, the good news is that it can be overcome. It doesn't have to control your ability to think and remember information. While it may take time, you can begin taking steps today to beat anxiety.

Just as your first hint that you may be struggling with anxiety comes from the physical symptoms, the first step to treating it is also physical. Rest is crucial for having a clear, strong mind. If you are tired, it is much easier to give in to anxiety. But if you establish good sleep habits, your body and mind will be ready to perform optimally, without the strain of exhaustion. Additionally, sleeping well helps you to retain information better, so you're more likely to recall the answers when you see the test questions.

Getting good sleep means more than going to bed on time. It's important to allow your brain time to relax. Take study breaks from time to time so it doesn't get overworked, and don't study right before bed. Take time to rest your mind before trying to rest your body, or you may find it difficult to fall asleep.

Along with sleep, other aspects of physical health are important in preparing for a test. Good nutrition is vital for good brain function. Sugary foods and drinks may give a burst of energy but this burst is followed by a crash, both physically and emotionally. Instead, fuel your body with protein and vitamin-rich foods.

Also, drink plenty of water. Dehydration can lead to headaches and exhaustion, especially if your brain is already under stress from the rigors of the test. Particularly if your test is a long one, drink water during the breaks. And if possible, take an energy-boosting snack to eat between sections.

Along with sleep and diet, a third important part of physical health is exercise. Maintaining a steady workout schedule is helpful, but even taking 5-minute study breaks to walk can help get your blood pumping faster and clear your head. Exercise also releases endorphins, which contribute to a positive feeling and can help combat test anxiety.

When you nurture your physical health, you are also contributing to your mental health. If your body is healthy, your mind is much more likely to be healthy as well. So take time to rest, nourish your body with healthy food and water, and get moving as much as possible. Taking these physical steps will make you stronger and more able to take the mental steps necessary to overcome test anxiety.

Mental Steps for Beating Test Anxiety

Working on the mental side of test anxiety can be more challenging, but as with the physical side, there are clear steps you can take to overcome it. As mentioned earlier, test anxiety often stems from lack of preparation, so the obvious solution is to prepare for the test. Effective studying may be the most important weapon you have for beating test anxiety, but you can and should employ several other mental tools to combat fear.

First, boost your confidence by reminding yourself of past success—tests or projects that you aced. If you're putting as much effort into preparing for this test as you did for those, there's no reason you should expect to fail here. Work hard to prepare; then trust your preparation.

Second, surround yourself with encouraging people. It can be helpful to find a study group, but be sure that the people you're around will encourage a positive attitude. If you spend time with others who are anxious or cynical, this will only contribute to your own anxiety. Look for others who are motivated to study hard from a desire to succeed, not from a fear of failure.

Third, reward yourself. A test is physically and mentally tiring, even without anxiety, and it can be helpful to have something to look forward to. Plan an activity following the test, regardless of the outcome, such as going to a movie or getting ice cream.

When you are taking the test, if you find yourself beginning to feel anxious, remind yourself that you know the material. Visualize successfully completing the test. Then take a few deep, relaxing breaths and return to it. Work through the questions carefully but with confidence, knowing that you are capable of succeeding.

Developing a healthy mental approach to test taking will also aid in other areas of life. Test anxiety affects more than just the actual test—it can be damaging to your mental health and even contribute to depression. It's important to beat test anxiety before it becomes a problem for more than testing.

Study Strategy

Being prepared for the test is necessary to combat anxiety, but what does being prepared look like? You may study for hours on end and still not feel prepared. What you need is a strategy for test prep. The next few pages outline our recommended steps to help you plan out and conquer the challenge of preparation.

Step 1: Scope Out the Test

Learn everything you can about the format (multiple choice, essay, etc.) and what will be on the test. Gather any study materials, course outlines, or sample exams that may be available. Not only will this help you to prepare, but knowing what to expect can help to alleviate test anxiety.

Step 2: Map Out the Material

Look through the textbook or study guide and make note of how many chapters or sections it has. Then divide these over the time you have. For example, if a book has 15 chapters and you have five days to study, you need to cover three chapters each day. Even better, if you have the time, leave an extra day at the end for overall review after you have gone through the material in depth.

If time is limited, you may need to prioritize the material. Look through it and make note of which sections you think you already have a good grasp on, and which need review. While you are studying, skim quickly through the familiar sections and take more time on the challenging parts.

Write out your plan so you don't get lost as you go. Having a written plan also helps you feel more in control of the study, so anxiety is less likely to arise from feeling overwhelmed at the amount to cover.

Step 3: Gather Your Tools

Decide what study method works best for you. Do you prefer to highlight in the book as you study and then go back over the highlighted portions? Or do you type out notes of the important information? Or is it helpful to make flashcards that you can carry with you? Assemble the pens, index cards, highlighters, post-it notes, and any other materials you may need so you won't be distracted by getting up to find things while you study.

If you're having a hard time retaining the information or organizing your notes, experiment with different methods. For example, try color-coding by subject with colored pens, highlighters, or post-it notes. If you learn better by hearing, try recording yourself reading your notes so you can listen while in the car, working out, or simply sitting at your desk. Ask a friend to quiz you from your flashcards, or try teaching someone the material to solidify it in your mind.

Step 4: Create Your Environment

It's important to avoid distractions while you study. This includes both the obvious distractions like visitors and the subtle distractions like an uncomfortable chair (or a too-comfortable couch that makes you want to fall asleep). Set up the best study environment possible: good lighting and a comfortable work area. If background music helps you focus, you may want to turn it on, but otherwise keep the room quiet. If you are using a computer to take notes, be sure you don't have any other windows open, especially applications like social media, games, or anything else that could distract you. Silence your phone and turn off notifications. Be sure to keep water close by so you stay hydrated while you study (but avoid unhealthy drinks and snacks).

Also, take into account the best time of day to study. Are you freshest first thing in the morning? Try to set aside some time then to work through the material. Is your mind clearer in the afternoon or evening? Schedule your study session then. Another method is to study at the same time of day that you will take the test, so that your brain gets used to working on the material at that time and will be ready to focus at test time.

Step 5: Study!

Once you have done all the study preparation, it's time to settle into the actual studying. Sit down, take a few moments to settle your mind so you can focus, and begin to follow your study plan. Don't give in to distractions or let yourself procrastinate. This is your time to prepare so you'll be ready to fearlessly approach the test. Make the most of the time and stay focused.

Of course, you don't want to burn out. If you study too long you may find that you're not retaining the information very well. Take regular study breaks. For example, taking five minutes out of every hour to walk briskly, breathing deeply and swinging your arms, can help your mind stay fresh.

As you get to the end of each chapter or section, it's a good idea to do a quick review. Remind yourself of what you learned and work on any difficult parts. When you feel that you've mastered the material, move on to the next part. At the end of your study session, briefly skim through your notes again.

But while review is helpful, cramming last minute is NOT. If at all possible, work ahead so that you won't need to fit all your study into the last day. Cramming overloads your brain with more information than it can process and retain, and your tired mind may struggle to recall even previously learned information when it is overwhelmed with last-minute study. Also, the urgent nature of cramming and the stress placed on your brain contribute to anxiety. You'll be more likely to go to the test feeling unprepared and having trouble thinking clearly.

So don't cram, and don't stay up late before the test, even just to review your notes at a leisurely pace. Your brain needs rest more than it needs to go over the information again. In fact, plan to finish your studies by noon or early afternoon the day before the test. Give your brain the rest of the day to relax or focus on other things, and get a good night's sleep. Then you will be fresh for the test and better able to recall what you've studied.

Step 6: Take a Practice Test

Many courses offer sample tests, either online or in the study materials. This is an excellent resource to check whether you have mastered the material, as well as to prepare for the test format and environment.

Check the test format ahead of time: the number of questions, the type (multiple choice, free response, etc.), and the time limit. Then create a plan for working through them. For example, if you have 30 minutes to take a 60-question test, your limit is 30 seconds per question. Spend less time on the questions you know well so that you can take more time on the difficult ones.

If you have time to take several practice tests, take the first one open book, with no time limit. Work through the questions at your own pace and make sure you fully understand them. Gradually work up to taking a test under test conditions: sit at a desk with all study materials put away and set a timer. Pace yourself to make sure you finish the test with time to spare and go back to check your answers if you have time.

After each test, check your answers. On the questions you missed, be sure you understand why you missed them. Did you misread the question (tests can use tricky wording)? Did you forget the information? Or was it something you hadn't learned? Go back and study any shaky areas that the practice tests reveal.

Taking these tests not only helps with your grade, but also aids in combating test anxiety. If you're already used to the test conditions, you're less likely to worry about it, and working through tests until you're scoring well gives you a confidence boost. Go through the practice tests until you feel comfortable, and then you can go into the test knowing that you're ready for it.

Test Tips

On test day, you should be confident, knowing that you've prepared well and are ready to answer the questions. But aside from preparation, there are several test day strategies you can employ to maximize your performance.

First, as stated before, get a good night's sleep the night before the test (and for several nights before that, if possible). Go into the test with a fresh, alert mind rather than staying up late to study.

Try not to change too much about your normal routine on the day of the test. It's important to eat a nutritious breakfast, but if you normally don't eat breakfast at all, consider eating just a protein bar. If you're a coffee drinker, go ahead and have your normal coffee. Just make sure you time it so that the caffeine doesn't wear off right in the middle of your test. Avoid sugary beverages, and drink enough water to stay hydrated but not so much that you need a restroom break 10 minutes into the test. If your test isn't first thing in the morning, consider going for a walk or doing a light workout before the test to get your blood flowing.

Allow yourself enough time to get ready, and leave for the test with plenty of time to spare so you won't have the anxiety of scrambling to arrive in time. Another reason to be early is to select a good seat. It's helpful to sit away from doors and windows, which can be distracting. Find a good seat, get out your supplies, and settle your mind before the test begins.

When the test begins, start by going over the instructions carefully, even if you already know what to expect. Make sure you avoid any careless mistakes by following the directions.

Then begin working through the questions, pacing yourself as you've practiced. If you're not sure on an answer, don't spend too much time on it, and don't let it shake your confidence. Either skip it and come back later, or eliminate as many wrong answers as possible and guess among the remaining ones. Don't dwell on these questions as you continue—put them out of your mind and focus on what lies ahead.

Be sure to read all of the answer choices, even if you're sure the first one is the right answer. Sometimes you'll find a better one if you keep reading. But don't second-guess yourself if you do immediately know the answer. Your gut instinct is usually right. Don't let test anxiety rob you of the information you know.

If you have time at the end of the test (and if the test format allows), go back and review your answers. Be cautious about changing any, since your first instinct tends to be correct, but make sure you didn't misread any of the questions or accidentally mark the wrong answer choice. Look over any you skipped and make an educated guess.

At the end, leave the test feeling confident. You've done your best, so don't waste time worrying about your performance or wishing you could change anything. Instead, celebrate the successful completion of this test. And finally, use this test to learn how to deal with anxiety even better next time.

Review Video: Test Anxiety
Visit mometrix.com/academy and enter code: 100340

Important Qualification

Not all anxiety is created equal. If your test anxiety is causing major issues in your life beyond the classroom or testing center, or if you are experiencing troubling physical symptoms related to your anxiety, it may be a sign of a serious physiological or psychological condition. If this sounds like your situation, we strongly encourage you to seek professional help.

Thank You

We at Mometrix would like to extend our heartfelt thanks to you, our friend and patron, for allowing us to play a part in your journey. It is a privilege to serve people from all walks of life who are unified in their commitment to building the best future they can for themselves.

The preparation you devote to these important testing milestones may be the most valuable educational opportunity you have for making a real difference in your life. We encourage you to put your heart into it—that feeling of succeeding, overcoming, and yes, conquering will be well worth the hours you've invested.

We want to hear your story, your struggles and your successes, and if you see any opportunities for us to improve our materials so we can help others even more effectively in the future, please share that with us as well. **The team at Mometrix would be absolutely thrilled to hear from you!** So please, send us an email (support@mometrix.com) and let's stay in touch.

If you'd like some additional help, check out these other resources we offer for your exam:
http://MometrixFlashcards.com/SOL

Online Resources

Due to our efforts to try to keep this book to a manageable length, we've created a link that will give you access to all of your online resources:

mometrix.com/resources719/vsolwhist2

It's Your Moment, Let's Celebrate It!

Share your story @mometrixtestpreparation